DR. JOE ANIELLO

Unconventional Essays
Suggesting How and Why
America Managed to Miss the
Boat on Doing "The Right Thing"

SUNKEN LEADERSHIP

Published by MindStir Media, LLC
45 Lafayette Rd | Suite 181| North Hampton, NH 03862 | USA
1.800.767.0531 | www.mindstirmedia.com
Printed in the United States of America.

ISBN-13: [0000000000000]

TABLE OF CONTENTS

DEDICATION

My Dear FRIEND and Colleague, Dr. Regina "Gina" Yanson.

She always prioritized the HUMAN first in Human Resources Management and lived a Beautiful, albeit too short, Life.

If you ever think that "Life is NOT Fair," she is heavenly proof of that.

I love you Gina just like everyone who ever met you!

"FORE!"-WARD

There are plenty of good books on Leadership. A few that have influenced me are: *"Servant Leadership." "Jesus Christ: CEO;" "Leadership Jazz;" "The Art of Leadership;"* and *"White Water Leadership."* These books are exceptionally good at informing and instructing about any and all aspects of the Discipline of Leadership. Therefore, my essays truly add little to that topic. Rather, I have focused on exploratory ideas that might explain some of the underlying causes in our Human Nature that may have inhibited the evolution of American Leadership that is necessary for the world of today and tomorrow. This, in an attempt to prompt some new and possibly different thoughts about those 'causes' that have produced a dearth of true Leadership amongst a plethora of 'symptoms' at this point in time.

I do not pretend to know any of these answers but merely to offer a possible direction from which to take further and future discussions.

About The Front Cover

The USS Constitution has been around almost as long as our Written Constitution. Both of these 'Icons' survive because despite innumerable 'attacks,' they remain indestructible. Even though the tall ship was made of wood, she is called "Old Ironsides" because of the way she was built. She was able to respond like an entirely different (much stronger) material. Likewise, the way our Constitution was written (built), our society was able to respond much stronger than normal individuals constructed in previous societies. There is nothing wrong with our written Constitution that cannot be rectified with Amendments nor with "Old Ironsides" for a new 'Captain' (POTUS?) to raise her back to the surface (symbolically), spruce her up and set sail again. Despite any and all differences that we may have, The "RIGHTS" detailed in our founding documents remain our collective strength and the secret to our future successes. This 'stuff' is inherently messy, but we must **NOT MAKE THE <u>MISTAKE</u> OF JUDGING OUR FOUNDING FATHERS' INTENTIONS/MOTIVATIONS/FALLIBILITIES 300 YEARS AGO THROUGH A <u>CURRENT</u> 'LENS'.** They did extraordinary work at that time, just as we need to do our own extraordinary work in the current context.

About the Back Cover

I know the world has become smaller and faster but that does not necessarily mean than we can never readjust our priorities as we go forward. When times are great, we can afford to have a bigger sphere of influence but when times are tough, it is very normal to "circle the wagons" and protect what is most precious. Maybe this is just another way to look at the United States of America with a slightly new perspective for the benefit of all legal American citizens first and foremost?

'OLD SCHOOL' Example:

"Perry Mason" - Manager

"Matt Dillon" - Leader

BLOG-A-DASIOUS ACKNOWLEDGEMENTS

A published author friend of mine suggested that I start a blog. Being a little old fashioned, I preferred to go a more "traditional" route and publish a book. I think of this as a kind of a blog on steroids. She was equally supportive of the book idea, and I acknowledge her as the best writer (and 'righter') I know, and as such, I thank Pam Johnson-Bennett for her inspiration and 50 years of family-like friendship.

After some academic 'research' I opted for the "hybrid" method of self-publishing with *The Manhattan Book Group*. As an author published in Academic Journals, I did not need a "ghost" writer; as a unique writing 'stylist,' I did not want a 'picky' editor and as a former Chief Marketing Officer, I wanted to have control over the Marketing of this 'product.'

My full gratitude goes out to Danielle Allan for all of her guidance in my decision process and the great folks at MBG/MINDSTIR who helped to make this dream a reality.

A special thanks for proofreading by my brother Tony "The Turtle" Aniello.

He has had a most successful life proving that "Slow and Steady Always Wins The Race."

He is the best Jerry, the Absolute BEST!

PERSONAL LEADERSHIP HALL OF FAME (EXPANDED MOUNT RUSHMORE)

Joseph Morcone (Physical)
96 year-old Maternal Grandfather

"Your Overall Health Is Your Greatest Wealth"

Anthony F. Aniello (Emotional)
Dad and Biggest Fan

"Your Own Inner Truth Can Beat The Entire World"

Albert Johnson (Spiritual)
The Original Ol' Professor

"Your Ultimate Freedom Is Having Few Requirements"

"Dr. (BIG) Wil" Clouse (Intellectual) Academic Advisor *Par Excellence*

"There Are Never A Shortage Of New Ideas BUT Most Of Them Are Found OUTSIDE of the 'Box'"

Dr. L. "Fred" Carter (Professional)
25 Years As President of Francis Marion University

"Active Listening Is Much More Important Than Talking"

INTRO-DEDUCTION

"Management is doing things right; Leadership is doing the right things."

-Peter Drucker

I do not think that anyone of any perspective at all would describe the current state of our United States of America as anything resembling a "Golden Age." As a matter of fact, it is far more likely the descriptions are one of "decline," "degeneration," "decadence," "descent," "disintegration," "DIS-Information," "disconnection," "discouraging," "devolution" or "dystopia." When did this begin and how in the hell did this happen? That is the trillion dollar question with a rapturous answer T.B.D.. An answer that I certainly do not have. Maybe the best I can do is offer some contrarian observations since doing the traditional and predictable has not seemed to move the Leadership 'needle' at all. This 'loss' has seemingly been imperceptible over a period of like eighty years. Much like the frog being unaware of the slow and gradual temperature increase in the pot of water on the stove, we seem to be just about 'cooked' when it comes to Leadership. The lesson here being that any 'transitions' without conscientiousness is fraught with dire consequences.

So, exactly WHAT has changed from the era of Leadership which made America 'great' in the world? When did "Management" start being completely separated from "Leadership" instead of the gateway for it? While Management has become almost a street smart necessity learned and practiced even before 18 years of age, true Leadership has become incredibly elusive and obsolescent if not virtually extinct. Since I was born in 1952, maybe I should begin proposing possible causes when my actual memory begins?

1950's

After the success from World War II, it seemed like everyone was suffering from a feeling of euphoria in that nothing seemed impossible or out of reach for the American Dreamers. What with the G.I. Bill underwriting unprecedented growth of higher education, house ownership, car ownership, vacation adventures and every modern convenience ever imagined, everybody was 'drunk' on the same magic potion. In retrospect, I guess we all got a little "fat, dumb and lazy" when it came to our collective assessment of reality. There had never been such a "middle class" in the history of the world, and it took a new type of "Leadership" to deal with that many people who had that much money. Followers soon realized WHAT their individual (and collective) votes now meant with much more power than they ever had before. I think life was just too easy for too many people in order for any new style of Leader/Leadership to emerge. Do not "rock the boat' and if "it is not broken no need to fix it." The 'independence' (noncompliance) of the new middle class happened much faster than anyone could anticipate or comprehend. Therefore, it was unlikely to "inspire" those people by Leading anyone anywhere from the delirious, delusionary, and happy place they were. In retrospect, Americans were asleep at the Leadership 'wheel.'

1960's

I think this was the first decade when people attempted to experiment with some new, post-war styles of Leadership. The issues fighting those attempts, unfortunately, were twofold. First, people like John F. Kennedy, Malcolm X, Robert F. Kennedy, and Martin Luther King were assassinated for their efforts. I do not think it really matters who killed these people nor how they were murdered. That treatise is for another book but the message to the country was infinitely clear, do NOT try Leading America to anything new or different! The second inhibitor of new Leadership was what I will lazily call, the "Hippie" movement. Aside from the long hair, different clothes, 'free' love and drug usage, there was a definite and expanded conscientiousness shift. People now dared to raise challenging questions about war, societal duty, Civil Rights, sex, work, money, the environment, and anything else that the Bible previously proclaimed as literally factual. For the purpose of these essays, it really does not matter if these changes were right or wrong; good or bad; healthy or unhealthy. It was just such a major change in society that the old rules of Leadership were of absolutely no use because they no longer did apply. Everyone just wanted to "Do their **own thing** MAN!" While it was invigorating for the "Generation of Flower Power," it was incredibly overwhelming for any prospective Leader to digest things so radical yet alone have any influence over this movement. This was also the time of the first 20th century war (Vietnam) which sharply divided our nation into two distinct sides. This division continues to this day with regards to America's role in wars outside of our own national boundaries. Hard to lead that way, is it not?

1970's

To me, the biggest impact of the "ME" Decade was Women's Liberation (**SHE** Decade?). Again, I have no interest or intention of formulating a judgement on any positive or negative values of this actualized 'movement' but rather how it may have made Leadership more complex and complicated. It certainly was a much more difficult adjustment for the reactive male population. The thing that is so ironic is that we now realize that Women typically are more naturally and better suited for Leadership qualities (supportive, nurturing, tolerant, empathic, patient, listening, etc.) than the majority of Men. Men are normally better suited for "Management" qualities (aggressive, goal oriented, tunnel visioned, calculating, less emotional, etc.). The issue here is that the Male species was not going to give up any Leadership position or opportunity without a really hard fight. Additionally, just because The Female species was now "liberated" it did not mean that the majority of them were automatically willing to immediately take over the reins of Leadership. That has been a slow and gradual process that continues to this day as Men kick and scream throughout the entire process. Women continue to prove themselves worthy and Men have learned that is can be better to be a great Manager than a poor Leader. Many men were unable or unwilling to "get in touch with" their 'feminine' side for Leadership positions. Traditional Women and Men also felt behind the 'eight ball' as a stay-at-home mother was not only viewed as "Old Fashioned" but also may have become a financial 'hardship' as a second salary was now needed to pay the bills. Many men now could no longer support (thereby feeling less potent) the entire family on only one salary which had been relatively reduced by the new (increased "supply") of women willing to work for <u>less</u> (decreased "demand") than their male counterparts. At this point, the split of Leadership began that exists to this day. Whether you call it "progressive" versus "conservative," Democrats vs. Republicans, or Christian vs. agnostic, there was no longer any one Leadership vision that applied to or appealed to much more than <u>any</u> half of the population.

1980's

Just as the nation was struggling with issues for Women, Aging, Disabilities, 'Orientations' and People of Color (after less serious previous struggles with religion and ethnicity), the era of "Globalization" descended upon the role of Leadership. I am not just referencing Legal Immigrants to America here (we have always had to deal with the assimilation of them), I am talking about a much "smaller and faster" world causing some important Leaders to forgo "America First" interests for any cheaper and/or more profitable ventures. (i.e. overseas manufacturing) No longer do 'northern' Leaders only have to motivate the "good ole boys" down south or descendants of our European 'ancestors' but are now faced with understanding an incredibly wider array of foreign cultures in people like varieties of Hispanics; diversities of Asians; and a very eclectic group of Africans/Middle-Easterners. We have proven that "Diversity" is a definite competitive advantage but that does not mean that all prospective Leaders can or will have success with such a wide variety of people any more than all baseball 'hitters' can be successful against a 100 mile-per-hour fastball pitch. The "wheat and chaff" of Leaders start getting separated during this decade and the 'secret' (if there is one) seems to being flexible and adaptable to the individual "behaviors" of the "Followers." Bottom line here is that the power had shifted significantly to the "Followers" and many Leaders had trouble accepting and adjusting to that shift. Technically, this is called the "Behavioral" Model of Leadership. This went against many of the beliefs that "bosses" had regarding (Authoritarian) Leadership roles and responsibilities so, many just dropped out from consideration and/or impact.

1990's

Up until now Leaders have only had the choice to either advocate for or exploit Human Nature. In this decade, the 'machines' enter into the 'equation' in a much greater and unavoidable manner. Technology explodes as a double-edged sword for business, government, politics, and the rest of civilization. Digitality may not have been the death knell of Leadership, but it certainly placed it on "life support." Especially if you consider qualities like honesty, trust, respect, loyalty, integrity, sincerity, and authenticity to be essential components of true Leadership. Those then become much less relevant when losing face-to-face contact with other people and/or in a contest with a machine's direct operation, memory, and speed. We are not against progress at all here but merely are saying that the impersonal nature of technology has made genuine Leadership (which requires personability) more elusive still. Just as athletes and entertainers whose efforts were sufficient in the 1950's might not be able to adequately compete against 1990's standards, the 'bar' of Leadership had been significantly raised. Consequently, one would never expect 1950's Leadership levels to be anywhere sufficient enough to deal with all these changes. For example, in the "good old days" followers heard a single, focused message about the values and policies that made the United States potentially great for ALL Americans. This message was reiterated in person by parents, relatives, teachers, clergy, first responders and 'legitimate' journalists. It is nearly impossible for those united Leadership 'voices' to compete with the constant barrage of hundreds of social media "influencers." The internet does not have to vet any of its information sources so, it is very tempting for people (especially naive younger people) to listen 'deafly,' and follow 'blindly' to nothing more than convincing opinions. It is really tough for any genuine Leader to compete with that. Whether by conscious choice or unconscious inability, technology has substantially shrunken the pool available of potential Leadership candidates in lieu of more follower self-sufficiency and gullibility.

21st Century

Some have postulated that it takes a "crisis" to truly bring out one's Leadership capacity (E.g., Winston Churchill, George "Dubya" Bush). Like the book says: "_Leadership is a Foul Weather Activity._" The hallmark of this century has been unprecedented and previously unthinkable events (9/11; The Great Recession; COVID) that have completely transcended (thus far) any Leaders' ability to make any great inroads in areas of World Peace, Legal Common Sense, Economic Prosperity, Political Ethics, Moral Dignity or Spiritual Enlightenment. The last half-century has certainly provided a lot of legitimate changes (mentioned above) to make an 'impossible' job even more difficult. Like Bruce Springsteen sang: "We are waiting for a savior to rise up from these streets" and why not? It has happened before although not very often. Christians have Jesus but most religions have their transformational Leaders. Rome had Cincinnatus just as most countries have their own salvation of Leadership. Baseball had Jackie Robinson, but most sports have their heroes to keep players chasing records. So, as we get more and more comfortable with crisis becoming the "new normal," what event might spur the revelation necessary for someone to don the next mantle of Transformational Leadership? It has never been harder but that was probably true for Jesus, Cincinnatus, and Jackie Robinson in their times as well. The difference is they did not experience the events mentioned above in the 60's, 70's, 80's, 90's, 00's and 10's to contend with. Here's hoping and praying that Artificial Intelligence (A.I.) is NOT that wolf (devil?) in sheep's clothing. I think the answer (without offering any specific solutions) might require a level of UN-selfishness not seen in a century, an unprecedented level of total human balance and an ultra-rare NON ego-centricity.

It's obvious to most everyone that our culture is really at a messy ebb. Karl Marx predicted that capitalistic societies would all 'topple' after about 500 years from the weight of human greed at its 'top'. It's up to all of us to prove him wrong. He does have a point in that, like a fish, a culture 'rots' from the head down. If we continue to replace basic human 'goodness' with conspicuous materialism, and human 'caring' with elevated self-importance, then the future will look bleak.

As a matter of inspiration, leaders have three major 'levers' to utilize. External Rewarding and Punishing can be used for short-term addictive results for minor issues. Intrinsic Inspiration can create longer-lasting and deep-seated changes in Followers. By far, the most powerful mechanism of influence is "Role Modeling." Our Leaders need to personally demonstrate the behavior they want their Followers to exhibit. They should take responsibility instead of blaming everyone and everything else. They need to act kindly, empathetically, and compassionately if they want their citizens to help each other. Collaboration, Cooperation, Communication, and Compromise must be goals at work in this day and age. Most importantly, they cannot be seen as unethical and/or immoral, if they want an honest, trusting, courteous and respectful society.

It has never been more difficult to inspire Followers than it is in our present world. Much like training cats is much harder than training dogs. We are left with a culture of 'cat-like' Followers so using dog tricks will not work very well. Cats, however, can be extremely rewarding members of our 'families' if you like intelligent, independent, self-sufficient, and incredible agile beings. This seems kind of like the current state of our citizenry. It does not benefit anyone to harken back to prior World War days when we treated homemakers, children, students, players, parishioners, and underlings like 'dogs.'

Here is just one example of how Leaders might consider a 'family'-type solution to a pressing world problem. Why not treat Taiwan like the British treated Hong Kong? Negotiate a ten-year, gradual return of "Formosa" back to Communist China. During that time, any and all Taiwanese can immigrate to the U.S., Canada, Japan, South Korea, the Philippines, Australia, New Zealand or anywhere else they want. Then they can bring with them all of their Silicone chip businesses and knowledge and we can avoid a potential World War III? A tough negotiation for sure. Is it not even worth a try? Who even talks about considering an attempt?…Anyone?...Bueller?

Those are the kind of Immigrants we need in America, not Mexican drug cartels. That idea is Leadership-"ish" because it recognizes the legitimate desires of China as well as our own for a much longer-term possible solution. Who wants to be ANY where that we are not wanted? We can just strengthen Japan, South Korea, The Philippines, and any other 'new' friends who want to willingly be on our "side." You can never hold people against their own will. Let them go and IF they come back to you it was meant to be and if NOT, you were never meant to have them in the first place.

While I have no blueprints for any plan nor any resumes of qualifications, I do know the theoretical definition of different types of Leaders, however. The BEST Leader acts on behalf of his/her organization in order to anticipate and prevent any crisis while visualizing/capitalizing on every opportunity before everyone else. A GOOD Leader can take immediate action to curtail any of his/her organizational crises once started and capitalize on every opportunity in a timely manner. A NON Leader allows bad things to happen to others in the organization while protecting him/herself and also capitalizes on every opportunity only for him/herself and those whom he/she 'owes.'

I hope and pray the following essays might strike the right 'chord' in some human Leadership 'messiah' out there.

PROSAIC LICENSE

If Management is thinking that your child is the cutest/smartest, then, Leadership is knowing how important it is that EVERY parent feels that way about theirs.

It must be due to my own mental limitations, but I just cannot find any simpler way to describe these current times without the necessity to combine a wide variety of references. (E.g., mixing metaphors).

Have you ever driven along a nice, gently winding road and noticed the lush and green foliage along the side of the road? If that lush, green foliage was Kudzu then, it might not be as nice as it appears superficially. For you see, beneath the surface of those thick, plentiful green leaves is a gradual process of suffocation, methodical elimination, and eventual extinction of what lies beneath. That is exactly the result of what the top 1% (elites) seem to be doing to the rest of the American people (and maybe the world) whether intentionally or unconsciously. Is it just the natural 'life cycle' for the rise and fall of every civilization or something more sinister?

It occurs to me that, in many ways, our current American culture (which, I care most about) is embroiled in a struggle of survival between the Kudzu juggernaut and the rest of the 'underbrush.' Coincidentally, it also bears a striking resemblance to and parallel with what the world was facing at the time when and a place where a man named Jesus walked the earth. People were then and are now addicted to immediate, tangible, shallow and sensory gratifications. The objects of desire may be different, but the 'disease' of addition is remarkably similar. That is to say, the weaknesses exploited by the powerful might eventually become the downfall of the addicted. It is a constant 'dance' of yielding to dangling temptations versus resisting those temptations.

At the center of these struggles is the intersection of our human nature and a divine nature. First off, let me state that I intend for this to be more philosophical than religious in perspective. It should not matter what your spiritual faith nor your political ideology to consider my point of view. 2,000 years ago, a man named Jesus 'suggested' that we might be better off in earthly life if we tried to be more like the Creator of the world and tried to resist the natural inclination to follow the instincts of the created. A peaceful, happy, and satisfying life would be the resulting reward and adding the possibility of an eternal afterlife (for a little extra motivation), might come about. Even if you do not believe the whole messiah, resurrection, heaven 'story,' experts in psychology and psychiatry probably concur that it is not such a bad way to deal with the challenges of this world. You know, the way that Jesus the philosopher and the teacher suggested regardless of any divine promises…Values like love thy neighbor, the golden rule, being a brother's keeper, turn the other cheek, etc. Or, at least, "Everything I ever really needed to know I learned in Kindergarten."

I guess it is just like the perennial struggle between the predator and its prey. On one hand, you have the exploiters of human nature (the few predators) and on the other hand, the meek and weak hordes of (God fearing?) prey just trying to elude the predator in order to survive another day. I once heard that the concept of religion was invented by the few 'rich westerners' (as opposed to eastern religions) in order to keep the many 'poor' from ganging together to kill the rich. (Thereby losing the 'golden' ticket to heaven via the 'sin' of murder). Imagine if the herd of wildebeest were able to coordinate an effort to work against the lion instead of being willing to sacrifice their young, old, and lame (like Humans routinely do). The lions would not have the same success record. Remember, "Let's roll" on the airliner headed for Washington D.C. on 9/11? Will the "meek" actually "inherit" the earth?

Maybe all the emphasis on analytics and statistics these days is just another name for the 'legalism' that predominated the Old Testament and with which Jesus had many 'issues'? I think it comes down to the fact that numbers, information, words, opinions or even laws can never be aggregated to summarize what it means to be a child of the universe. Yet, we let the predators do exactly that as they over-grow the underbrush with their 'planted' kudzu. I told you that, I would intentionally and unavoidably mix metaphors!

You have probably heard that there are lies, damn lies and research. Despite being a college professor with an "earned" doctorate, I am here to tell you that, these predators can pretty much provide data to 'prove' any darn thing that they are 'selling.' I think the same goes for the preponderance of lawyers, authors, publicists, politicians, and media spin-doctors. At least the pimps are more honest about what they <u>actually</u> do. We must never forget that all of these self-serving so-called 'facts' ("fake news") have truly little correlation to authentic knowledge, sincere wisdom, or one's own genuine truth.

Now for a word about narcissism and the narcissists. As someone once said, one has either to **believe** in God or to BE their own God. Never has this arrogance seemed to be more true. The anti-Christ might not be a person at all but the miss-use and abuse of technology (I.e., social media). Humility has become a lost art as somehow most people audaciously believe that <u>their</u> opinions, <u>their</u> pictures, <u>their</u> branding, <u>their</u> image, <u>their</u> daily routines, and <u>their</u> mere existence is cause for attention/celebration. Just as a black belt in martial arts does not have to pick fights to prove toughness (but a bully does), it seems pathetic to me that so much time and energy is wasted on digital publication in an attempt to 'prove' the unnecessary and mediocre. ("reality T.V." anyone?)

To me, it would seem best that humans spend (a lot of) work on internal growth and development, not on attempting to dominate external minutia. Listen, I know it is <u>all</u> about the money, I am no dummy. Have you heard about the research (D. Kahneman), however, that 'proves' that true happiness can only be increased on personal income up to $75,000/per year (adjustable for geography and size)? Any amount more than that will NOT contribute appreciably to one's individual life satisfaction, just their accumulation of 'things.' Money is better at reducing sadness than increasing happiness. See, I also know how to play the research 'game.'

How about today's moneychangers, do you recognize them? They are the egomaniacal purveyors of fantasy (lotteries?) designed to escape the challenging work of living and to provide bogus answers to the naïve, uninformed, trusting, and gullible. Money is the answer, now what is the question? To me the 'superheroes' predominating movies, video games, television and print are not much different from Greek/Roman mythological gods or biblical parables/miracles. They have the effect of a type of 'hypnosis' thereby preventing people from thinking for themselves and to willingly line up for big 'manipulations.' By vicariously identifying (and escaping) with these, unrealistic portrayed personas (including 'divas' and 'divos'), we can avoid the need to look inward and find our appropriate place in the world.

Something pathetic happens when smart, individual people congregate together into groups…they seem to get foolish. Have you heard the one about a horse designed by committee comes out looking like a camel? Well, when people with good common sense (which should be enough) gather into herds, hoards or crowds only dreadful things happen (act like jackasses?). They are led from the pasture to the corral, get slaughtered (figuratively) or at least end up hurting each other. Maybe that is why Jesus is portrayed as a "shepherd?" Sheep only give up their wool but keep their lives. Chickens, Pigs and Cattle are not so 'blessed.' That is exactly what the power brokers want…voluntary congregation for ease of control (by keeping most people in the 'dark'?). Here is another one: "No one ever went broke UNDER-estimating the collective wisdom of the American consuming public." It was okay to have more money than brains when the economy was lifting everyone but as things get tighter, people will have to learn discipline, deferred gratification, and restraint…somehow. During America's 'golden' economic age, the 'ride' was like hanging on for dear life on a runaway stallion. Now, it is more like a trail ride through mud upon an old nag.

The world needs more 'good shepherds' ("Leaders") to provide for and protect the masses/commoners. (I.e., having only to give your hair, not your hide). I just do not see any great flock 'tending' this day. I do not see many "states people" or diplomats from our elected officials despite <u>that</u> being their primary duty and responsibility. Wealth has the negative consequence of putting one out of touch with most people's reality as it insulates by creating one's own 'comfort' barrier. There is a classic "out-of-touch" story about President George Bush not knowing what a bar code scanner was because he had NEVER been to a store. I realize most roles are becoming increasingly pressurized and stressful but in addition to poor governing ("public service" my ass, not at those total compensation & graft packages), I also do not see enough proper leadership of many other positions of authority from parents; educators; athletics; healthcare; journalists; clergy, etc. Therefore, how do we bring about good shepherd Leadership when a gaggle of manager-qualified organizations guides us?

I am not much of an historian but there is one thing about the Roman Empire that has always stuck with me, even decades after learning about it. With all of the wonderful freedoms allowed in their democracy, the Romans believed that there are times that **inertia** can result when two or more sides 'pull' in opposite directions with an equal degree of force. During those times, the government will put their 'differences' aside and will call for a "benevolent despot" to make the necessary decisions. The idea is that this person will make the BEST decision for MOST people given the realities of the situation and circumstances. Not the PERFECT decision, not one that satisfies EVERYONE but what NEEDS to be done. The thinking here is that inaction and the time/energy/resources wasted on debating is actually WORSE than ANY choice that is made. The Benevolent Despot that I remember best was Cincinnatus who gave everyone enough to be satisfied and comply with what was best for the state.

The tendency of today's 'managers' is to react/respond only <u>after</u> disaster strikes. You mean to tell me that the high six-figure vice-president for American Airlines security never thought to install locks on airplane cockpit doors BEFORE September 11? Did any NYC Fire Chief think about a long fire hose with one pumping end in New York Harbor and the other end attached to a hose nozzle on a helicopter 80 floors up in the sky? What did those 'leaders' do to earn their salaries, close the barn door after the horse escaped? Did the CIA talk to the FBI BEFORE the Department of Homeland Security was created? My advice is to initiate corrective actions <u>before</u> things reach crucial proportions. I.e., do not let the "perfect" get in the way of the "good." Without a collective willingness to make small sacrifices systematically along our way, we leave ourselves with no choices but the ones that history has chronicled as causing devastating tragedies in human devolution. Like war, genocide, famine, plague, holocaust, revolution, etc...

Some examples of making the helpful changes might be a.) NOT supporting excessive levels of greed by those 'influencers' of society. Specifically: I would like to know the exact financial incentives given to our celebrity spokespeople and product endorsers. Likewise for media personalities who might have strong reasons for 'shading' ("perception is reality") a story one-way or the other. b.) I think we should have the widely disseminated disclosure of exactly how much/what charitable causes that millionaires/billionaires support. After all, the rest of us subsidize all of the tax-deductible contributions of wealthy people. I would at least like to know exactly which issues/influences that I am 'unwillingly' supporting. c.) If you want to put America first, how about a different tax schedule for those who contribute to domestic (greater deduction) causes versus foreign causes? d.) Here is an idea whose time has come thanks to technology. I want to indicate to my governmental representatives exactly what percentage of my taxes to spend on the programs (E.g., defense, education, environment, crime, etc.) that I prefer. The same right should exist for every other taxpayer in proportion to taxes paid (one dollar paid, one vote). I can do it for the United Way, why not for the United States? It certainly would make interesting reading for the constituents and an indicative 'scorecard' of an individual's legislative voting performance.

Right now, it is "buyer beware" with regard to every second of our existence (which is overwhelming for all but a few). It is very random when we hear of a doctor recommending (debatable) tests from the laboratory that he/she owns. It is also very seldom when the questionable ethics of university grant-supported 'research' is exposed thereby confirming a pharmaceutical company's desired results after contributing said grant. Additionally, when a Ph.D. in psychology receives exorbitant consultancy fees to advise advertising agencies which insecurity 'buttons' to push in order to encourage 'chubby' teenage girls to smoke rather than eat; lest they never find a 'prince' to marry them (the pervasive Disney effect). The reality is that these 'predators' are smart as hell, motivated (unethical?) as all get out and use consumer behavior psychology like a weapon to place trusting 'customers' into a compliant 'trance.' I am not even blaming these people *per se,* but I am expecting more morality out of the 'loophole' makers. Or at least the loophole closers.

It may be time to change the 'rules' of the "American Dream"? I am a huge proponent of the 'bell' curve. This seems to be the perfect paradigm to detail the normal distribution of natural phenomena. In other words, how human scientists can explain universal laws (or God's plans if you prefer). It is always a 'red' flag to me when too much of any kind of 'activity' happens at either end of the bell 'tails' (standard deviations). The challenge for all of us as individuals is that the 'world' wants us to exist in the extremes because that is where we are most easily manipulated into circumstances which benefit the 'kudzu.' Healthy balance is its own reward and is very much an individual responsibility. I acknowledge that it is extremely hard to stand strong against the worldly forces, which pull us towards the 'quick and easy' (end tail) solutions away from our normal and natural (best for each individual) struggles of existing; let alone growing and developing.

We are living in a time when this Bell Curve model work so well for the concept of "power." Every day, the news reminds us how it is equally bad to have too much power, as it is to have too little power. It is the rare instance when someone with no power can rise out of that powerless condition even to be heard yet alone influence. Conversely, I am still waiting for someone to resist the tremendous temptation pressure not to have (mostly his) or her absolute power to corrupt absolutely. (Self-restraint is the true 'measure' of "Character"?) Here is a thought: As long as powerful people still have material possessions to pursue, maybe they are not as likely to abuse others (E.g., sexually) as seems to be happening now. In other words, on the materialism/sexual power continuum, when some people's possessions accumulation 'container' is completely full, there may be no other possessions to pursue other than the power over another's own sexual possession (Jeffrey Epstein)? For some, not all, it just might be an individual's own "tipping point." This is one reason that legalized Prostitution might need to be Re-evaluated on a national scale.

IT'S ONLY HUMAN NATURE (BUT I KNOW IT)

*If Management is making sure that
YOU get through that long stop light then,
Leadership is making sure that
YOU do not hold up others before it turns "red" again.*

Most of all of the pundits, prophets, politicos, and profiteers throughout the ages always seem to proffer up solutions to ALL of mankind's problems from 'outside' remedies rather than at the root source of the issue…from within. The proverbial 'Band-Aid' answer. To me, the reason for such strategies and implementations is obvious, the ease of the 'sale.' That sale is dependent on both the good side and the bad side but mostly the indelible side of Human Nature. The exploiters and the exploited; the predators and the prey; the shrewd and the gullible; the manipulators and the naïve; the entitled and the humble; the takers and the givers as well as the capable and the incapable.

Only by understanding and accepting Human Nature (OUR own in the context of total Humanity) can anyone hope to have even a 'puncher's chance of building the most successful life for ourselves. Maybe those individuals who seem to 'win' at life are better at the 'game' of Human Nature? You know, like P.T. Barnum said: "there's a sucker born every day." Was he really such an intelligent, innovative, and 'special' person with his whole circus idea? I think his biggest advantage was knowing that most people have such a lazy approach to the 'inside' of their own being/life that they will believe almost anything to escape the 'reality' of themselves. Same goes for Ripley and any other 'freak' shows that attract the insatiable morbid curiosity of Human Nature. Most people would rather go to the museum or gallery and see what the so-called experts define as "beauty" rather than take the time, energy, and painful self-growth to become their own type of "artist" and define it for themselves.

The same can be said for all of the sports entertainers, music entertainers, theatre entertainers, dance entertainers, etc. The "lazy" aspect of Human Nature would rather watch (and pay for) a dedicated 'performer' than participate themselves. I do not think that fact has ever changed to this point of the "Race's" evolution. I see absolutely no relevant difference between the Roman Colosseum contests and the WWE. Both (and every other) is playing to the "vicarious" component of our Human Nature. Most of us would rather watch the Tour de France than bicycle around the neighborhood with our friends/family. Which does us the most good? At the very least, it protects us from confronting our own limitations while keeping alive any illusions that we want to maintain. I think the organizers, promoters, sponsors, merchandisers, and media of every event have figured that out pretty well, don't you? Same goes for the Master's Golf Tournament, America's Got Talent, The Oscars, Emmy's, Tony's, Grammy's, World Series, NBA Playoffs, The Kentucky Derby and in spades, The Super Bowl. Partial list…agreed?

The basic principle at work here is that, since the beginning of recorded time, people have not been able to resist the 'temptation' of the external 'fruits' (Garden of Eden) they will substitute for the much harder internal work that the Creator seems to have intended for each one of us; to be done on <u>our own</u>. The 'devilish' minority of those among us have never stopped using this component of Human Nature to enrich themselves at the expense of the naïve, gullible, and trusting majority. Maybe that is the only real difference that separates us anyway, you know, the tempters and the tempted? The unchanging Human decision of taking the 'easy' way out and following the path of least resistance. For purposes of this, I will classify "organized religion" (reminding us the **only** difference being, 'salvation' as a 'sold' product/service) as part of the Human Nature category and <u>not</u> part of anyone's own concept of a 'Divine' (truly spiritual) Nature.

At the risk of over-simplification, could it be that, for the most part, Human Nature is trying to "get by" from extrinsic sources while Divine Nature is meant for us to "get better" through intrinsic work?

Please do not misunderstand me here, I am not trying to say that Human Nature is either good or bad, it is just what it is…Human and <u>not</u> Divine. All of the things that each generation throughout history thinks are changing have no more effect on Human Nature than a change of clothes has on the real shape of one's body. Yet, we become so enamored with the significance of those 'apparent' changes just as we become delusional, dedicated followers of 'fashion.' Human Nature wants to be easily fooled by the superficial illusions of a 'magic' trick (spoiler alert-the Statue of Liberty does not really disappear) or the unnatural appearances of an animal in a zoo and **not** have to face the hard reality of the truth (I.e., cruel animal imprisonment for our Amusement). We are put on this earth to become more Divine, even in the slightest bit. That is why the idea of reincarnation has such a strong logical appeal to me. Examining the snail-in-molasses progress we make here on earth; it is impossible for me to think that any one of us would really deserve a trip to <u>any</u> "Divine" 'heaven' in **only** ONE lifetime. Okay, maybe Saint (Mother) Teresa? :o)

Just to repeat here, I am not judging Human Nature but merely trying to explain its inherent limitations which may shed some light upon some new ways of dealing with it. The crux of the matter would seem to rest squarely on the concept of "subjectivity." By definition, there is absolutely no Human Being who cannot escape their <u>one and only</u> ability (extremely limited) to subjectively perceive. When I was single, I had a preference of being attracted to blonde women (not unique I know but having grown up in an Italian neighborhood, they were a 'novelty' not experienced until high school; remember TV was black & white then). Looking back, I was so "subjective" that, I would prefer a less-pretty blonde over a more-pretty brunette! A well-educated, good friend and I would often commiserate about the perils of being single in our 'circumstances.' The example of "subjectivity" here is that she lectured me about limiting (deluding) myself tremendously with my "blonde-only" attraction. Yet, the irony here is, she would ONLY date African American men (she is Caucasian) but she could not see her "limitation" (only MINE) of HER OWN preference ("oh, that is different" she would decry). Calling all Kardashians!

Truthfully, we can only see ourselves and the entire rest of the world from ONE vantagepoint, our own(Bounded Rationality). What an incredible handicap! Even the most empathic among us can only 'guess' at any 'feeling' other than our own (even that is incredibly hard) by using senses woefully inadequate for anyone other than ourselves. Our eyes can only look without, not within. Our ears can only hear though a very narrow sound frequency. We can only speak words from a limited vocabulary of approximated comprehension. (maybe why advanced alien beings are always portrayed as communicating telepathically?) Our senses of smell and taste are finely filtered through our brain's understanding of its experience. Finally, our sense of touch has proven to be inferior to many classes of so-called "lower" animals, not just other mammals. In fact, there are 'animals' who are better with EACH AND EVERY of our senses than Humans. Eagle's sight; Dog's smelling; Dolphin's hearing, etc., etc.

The second "common denominator" for me here is, each person's own EGO. I really do not believe that our ID has changed that much over time. Our ID is derived from our existence as a Human "animal" and our basic needs and physiological urges to survive and reproduce seem perpetual. Maybe the manner in which we satisfy those 'hungers' and 'thirsts' changes with resource quantity/quality availability, fads, and trends but at its core, it remains pretty constant. Excess is still excess as it was for Caligula and Henry the VIII. Scarcity is still scarcity as it was for the Pilgrims' first winter and the children of Biafra. I also do not think that there has been much change either in our SUPER EGO, even before it was known as such. Whether or not there is an inherent "conscience" in all of us or not, there seems to be almost universal agreement throughout history as to what has been taught to be good, or bad, positive, or negative and healthy or unhealthy. Whether those lessons have been the purview of organized religion or not, all Humans (even atheists) are at least exposed to those differences at an early age and the construction of their own SUPER EGO (and its faith) regardless of whether they chose to adhere to them or not. We all understand inherently what we know to be "right or wrong."

As it applies to the concepts of laws, morals, and ethics, those might very well be the construct of the collective EGO and we need to address that next. So, bear with me here, if the ID is the left/lower 'tail' of the Human Nature Bell Curve and the SUPER EGO is the right/upper 'tail,' that leaves us a whole hell of a lot of room (like 80%) to place each individual's EGO under the Bell of the curve. That is precisely the question <u>and</u> the answer to success and/or failure of Human Nature. We cannot escape the <u>narrow</u> predicament of our own "subjectivity" and conversely, there is **so much** room within our own EGO development that we either: reach our maximum Human capacity or get ourselves in really big trouble. It is incredibly challenging for each person to navigate the strong, polar-opposite pulls of our bodily desires and the allegiant demands of our 'souls.' For the insecure, everyone and everything else might seem better and more deserving and consequently, the person of 'small' EGO might struggle with satisfying their own (reasonable) needs and wants. On the other extreme, the narcissist might feel so entitled that, he/she possesses an excessive distortion of what share of life's 'blessing's they want or need (I.e., what they "deserve"), at the exclusion of ANY God-ly influences.

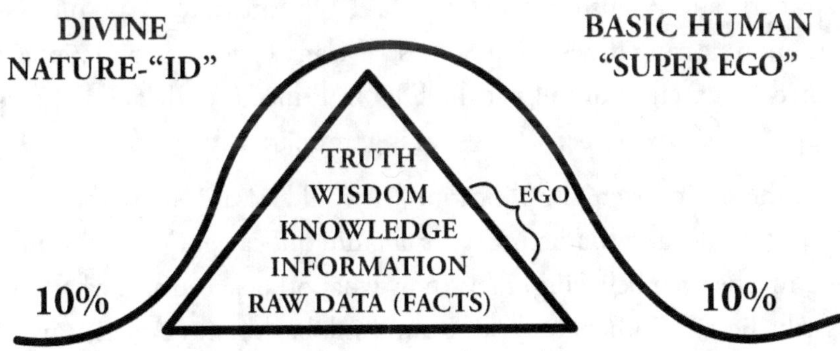

The above 'pyramid' has always been a good paradigm for me in terms of describing the individual EGO regarding varying levels of 'healthy' versus 'unhealthy' along a 'vertical' continuum. Now what the hell do I mean by that? Taking a person who exclusively deals in Factual Data, I might suggest that person's world (subjective perception) is mostly 'black & white' whereby he/she has a large sense of self-importance (closer to ID). I am not saying that is all bad although "Data" does NOT leave much room for "gray" explanations/understanding/interpretations nor many opportunities for a Divine influence. Someone once said that you either: "Have to believe in God or be your own God." Any person at the bottom of this pyramid is where the largest EGO's of Human Nature operate. (spoiler alert – the smallest EGO's reside at the top of the pyramid closest to Divine Nature).

Some non-United States people have called us the "Ugly American," "Highly Arrogant," "Wasteful," "Overly Litigious," "Selfish," "Self-Righteous," "Excessive," etc. Trying to keep more of a Global citizenship, I can see how others would think/feel/believe that. After all, our collective EGO has informed most of our decisions and policies not only domestically but around the world. I think we come by it honestly with our WASP (conquer the world by taking its best resources) and misogynistic heritage. Look at the English language as compared to other 'tongues.' Because it was meant for the elites, it is deliberately, inconsistent of pronunciation and its "properness" is out of reach for many without formal education. Also look at our measure of "standardized" intelligence, not all 8 or so types of Multiple Intelligence (E.g., "Emotional Intelligence") but limited to Math (numbers) and English (words); I.e., SAT-type measures. I am quite sure that upon hearing the Rolling Stones, "I Can't Get No Satisfaction," the immediate reaction of folks at the ETS in Princeton NJ (and their tight 'poop chutes') would be: "Why, that is grammatically incorrect!" :-D

At the risk of over "simplification," I would hazard to say that a lot of successful Sales and Marketing types fall into this category. Those thinking (and maybe even believing) they know what others need and what is necessarily 'best' for others to want. I can think back to my Advertising days when, one prominent New York agency had for its slogan: "Truth Well Told." This was a clever way of saying that we can and will use lies, damn lies and research ("Data") right up unto the 'line' of litigation liability (and many have crossed that line – see FTC records). Were they smart, safe, and successful? Mostly yes! Was it a constant clash of titan EGO's? Absolutely yes! In fact, for these EGO-maniacs (narcissists?), their ID's are never too far out of reach. Did they ever consider consumers' ability to 'afford'? That might get in the way of their massive earning potential. Were they God fearing? Not so much.

Weighing in with slightly smaller EGO's (but still pretty significant) are the "Information" processors. Somewhere along the line of aggregating "Raw Data," a more 'open' person might allow for the rare occasion when 1 + 1 = 3. This normally cock sure (by-the-number's) person might be willing to allow for that occasional exception (not the rule) where something new can be discovered via the "unexplained." Keeping one's EGO in check or at least subject to an honest doubt every once in a "blue moon" might always be a possibility. At the risk of further "generalization," I might see many political types (law-yer, where "yer" is defined as "instead of 'love'"!) falling in this category although the political 'machinery' often 'manipulates' rather than purely 'aggregates' the Data (E.g., "fake news"). Also, we might find many professional athletes being classified in this manner. Most are "measured" by their performance statistics (processed "analytics"), and I suppose, one cannot help but feel 'superior' when one can do something that so **few** others can (E.g., dunk a basketball). Self-Esteem is certainly at work full-time among these folks as they cannot help but think that they are more 'valuable' to the world than most.

The 'middle ground' EGO allows for both the predictable AND the random in their rabid pursuit of "Knowledge." Without that, nothing really meaningful ever happens for them. They want to make their 'mark' by applying information in a manner in which something 'improves' in a pragmatic way. It is not a meaningful endeavor for these types of EGO's unless all the effort leads to some practical 'action.' I am thinking about investigative reporters and/or police detectives here. Just enough EGO to be "right" in their evaluation but not so much that negates the "public service" element. Additionally, we might assign most graduate-school-level professionals to this middle ground, E.g., Doctors – both Medical and Academic. In general, the intrinsic motivation of "achievement," "accomplishment," "responsibility," and "self-worth/esteem/development" drives this group more than just money, title, position, status, external recognition, and prestige.

We have now past the halfway point of Human Nature EGO's and have turned just slightly toward the ideal (however, unattainable in this lifetime) Divine destination. That small group of Humans with whom we associate "Wisdom." For them, the emphasis here has to be subjugating one's own EGO to the prospects of the ambiguous and the uncertain. There very well may be a strong need to know but they are looking at life through a telescopic lens rather than a microscopic one. I would say that it takes a lot of courage to develop the perspective and context to see things in a "Wise" proportion. So many of these lives become trading high percentage risks for low percentage payouts. These folks are willing to take that chance. I would guess that most of these people are motivated to "leave the world in a better place than they found it." This is such a minority position as most of us would rather keep the "devil we know" than venture into the UN-known. The wise person is willing to continually do battle with his/her EGO and does not ALWAYS win but is NEVER afraid of the outcome. I often see Entertainment types (commercial and fine Artists) in this arena. After all, there is NO Business like Show Business! I think the best performers often recognize and realize, something 'greater' than themselves (a "muse") has contributed substantially to their success and quite often acknowledge that (humility) in public acceptance speeches. Certainly, Leaders from all walks of life fit this description.

What can be said about an EGO life which continuously attempts to deal with all aspects and facets of the "Truth"? The EGO is a **non-factor** in the lives of the "Truth" seekers. While not quite Divine, they certainly bump up against that realm at the top of this pyramid. We even have earthly names for them do we not? We call them demigods, saints, angels, starving artists, and martyrs. At the very least, these folks seem in awe of life and constantly practice humility. They have seen the 'light' in their "calling" but have no interest in convincing the rest of us of ANYTHING or one-upping ANYBODY. It is a silent confidence and conviction of what they know to be their <u>own</u> "Truth" and they can easily and often become overwhelmed or even overcome by their 'blessings.' Maslow calls this the "Self-Actualization" stage in his Hierarchy. When lesser mortals come in contact with them, we take note of the differences in their authenticity, sincerity, honesty, and genuineness. Theirs is a "goal standard" (since "gold" has NOT been our most precious metal in quite some time) which serves as an example and an aspiration but seems somehow unattainable for the vast majority of us.

So, what is the lesson to be learned here for anyone that fancies themselves a student of Human Behavior and/or is a People Person? First of all, accept the reality of Human limitations in that, we only can see things from our own point of view. I.e. - There are always 3 views: Yours, Mine and the REAL one. That usually strongly incorporates WIIFM? (what is in it for me?). Even people whom we altruistically call the "Givers" are in fact, doing the giving for THEMSELVES and their own Need satisfaction. It also seems 'natural' for individuals to want to associate with the **highest** status group that one can. Sometimes, African Americans such as Michael Jordan or Tiger Woods have been criticized by some for not being "black enough." It seems easier to be "Black" or "Italian" or "Jewish" when you are NOT a Billionaire. Once one attains that rarified status, one becomes a member of the much more important and exclusive (Billionaire Club) "minority." This is much like other minorities (Hall-of-Famer; US Senator; Olympic Gold-Medal winner; Miss America; former Marine; Oscar-winner, etc.) which trumps ANY other social class along the EGO hierarchy. All of our EGO's propel us towards the 'highest' societal level in which we can be classified. Maybe that is why so-called "aristocratic"-types can have distain for the *nouveau riche* category? For "Blue Bloods," more money is such a crude (EGO) measure of self-worth as compared to more humble, understated, and closer-to-the-Divine(?) criteria.

Understanding, comprehension and most of all acceptance can only emanate from the place where any individual is "coming from" (the Hippies tried that in the 1960's). That place is made up of a unique set impressions, experiences, and expectations as derived from the collective total minutes (good, bad, and indifferent) of his/her life. It cannot be duplicated or ever fully identified. Therefore, start from the other person, ("them"), when beginning any interaction and be THE person to put oneself in THEIR place and attempt to walk a "mile in THEIR shoes." While imperfect as hell, it is the best option available as opposed to expecting THEM to do all the hard 'work.' To paraphrase a well-worn cliché, "All You Need is Love," the meaning here quite simply being that *AGAPE* Love really can be one's best tool for all of the understanding necessary to conquer all of life's petty details which consume most people. Remember, "small" people obsess about **other** people; "average" people focus on life's events; while "Divine-aspirant" people devote themselves to ideas to help others. As difficult as this is, it is still easier than the next step.

The next step was best expressed by Quincy Jones while producing the seminal record for "Live Aid" (raising money for starving people in Africa). He merely said to all of the superstar artists participating in the recording: "Please check your EGO at the door!" (in order to become a vital part of something bigger than themselves). As hard as it might be to see things from another's perspective, suppressing our own sense of reasoning and logic can seem UN-Human. If we add to this rationalizing the aspects of instinct and/or intuition, our resolve to be 'right' and to have our own way, is almost insurmountable for all but the most enlightened/evolved.

As previously described, I realize that the entire concept of EGO is on a "sliding scale" (80% continuum) but suffice to say that the **more** that people feel 'invested' in their particular position or point-of-view, the more they gravitate down towards the Human "Data." Consequently, the harder it then becomes to see the "Truth" from the view approaching (but never reaching) the Divine. It certainly takes that 'special' player to want to take the last basketball shot or to have 'ice water' run through one's arteries to make a seven-foot putt when the difference between making and missing is $500,000. Likewise, it takes that same special rarity to place aside one's EGO and rise above any mere mortal actions/reactions. Aside from "Truth," everything else is really just "opinion."

Certainly, the current cultural influences/pressures are working **against** keeping one's EGO in check. For one, Social Media, (as well as "Reality TV and the Talent 'lottery' shows), have created an inflated sense of self-im-portance (I.e., EGO) in comparison to any attention given to the Divine/Super Ego. I remember hearing about a survey of Millennials, the majority of whom, would rather be "famous" for something "notorious" than NOT being "famous" at all. Talk about an EGO problem! The Social Media have convinced many normally God-fearing, Authority-listening people to con-vert into the 'devils' that, somehow believe their 'butthole' (everyone has one and they ALL stink) opinions, their artificial images, their unimportant accomplishments, and any mediocre visual technology is somehow much more significant that it really is. I think this can be traced directly back to the "participation" trophy culprits. This entire fascination by the onlookers and the addiction by the providers has done nothing but distort the role of ones' EGO through a steady diet of the "ID" while forcing any conscious sensibilities (Super Ego) to the permanent 'back burner.'

Right along with the current sense of self-entitlement (note how much of Advertising implores everyone to: "get what YOU deserve") is the need for "immediate gratification." There is hardly any ability of anyone to de-lay or defer said gratification until at which time it has been "earned." Or, at least until some (God's) "perfect timing" as determined by something other than us (absence of Divinity) or salespeople. The truth is in fact that yes, EVERYONE wants EVERYTHING "fast" (yesterday), "inexpensive" (cheap) and "correct" (right) but the reality is in fact, ANYONE can only have TWO-OUT-OF-THREE of any of these at any **one** TIME. If it is Fast and Cheap, it will <u>not</u> be Correct! If it is Fast and Correct, it will <u>not</u> be Cheap! If it is Cheap and Correct, it will <u>not</u> be Fast!

The easy part was talking about it. I went through all this for the second easiest part: awareness. That is about all I can do to help. The rest is a highly individualized self-evaluation and decision to see oneself differently. One has to believe all of this specific stuff and then be highly motivated to make the conscious choice and finally, to stick with that choice when it becomes really hard and seems to make truly little sense (faith). I remember my "wisest" friend telling me when we were both 20 years old that: "Love is a Choice!" Back then, I thought "love" was some magic dust sent into the air from Disneyland or something. I wanted the easy, fairytale way to LOVE yet HE was wise enough to know that something as precious and rare does not come easy but requires a lot of hard 'inside' work. It will never be the simple, outside manner in which the world was trying to market/sell it to us. He was wise at a much younger age than me when he said: "Love is a Choice." And THAT requires a lifetime of really hard internal work.

I realize it is a bit presumptuous to talk about "Human Nature" in such general terms but that was the point of this treatise. As a true student of the subject and hopefully, as a successful practitioner of the phenomenon, one would expect each individual to make any necessary modifications for her/his own "subsets." Aside from the common components of which I have written, factors such as gender, age, race, and nurture (E.g., class) would certainly produce some relatively minor variations. Just like an apple is always an apple but there are a number of varieties to distinguish them and differences to consider whether making cider or a pie. I, for one, would expect the "expert" of the orchard to know that, understand that, and make any necessary distinctions.

Do not expect to absorb one's own concept of the "Divine" from any religious organization. They might be able to help a little but it is a long and lonely journey that one must make alone. It takes the commitment, dedication, and the willing devotion to believe in one's own highest nature. Fully expect your EGO to **<u>fight</u>** you each and every step along the way since its very existence is to 'survive' by explaining/excusing itself about ALWAYS being "right." The EGO is more **Rationalizing** that <u>Rational</u>; more **Justifying** than <u>Logical</u>; and more **Generalizing** than <u>Accepting</u>.

Also, never discount the "Economic Survival" motive that can inform and explain much of 'crazy' Human Nature (on 'steroids' in the USA). For example, the "Tell All" books written (E.g., Tiger Woods' caddie) after the fact of gainful employment at the expense of gratitude and loyalty for the person written about. Like the saying goes: "if you ever want to understand the REAL reason for something, just follow the money." Also, "money is THE answer; now what is the question"? Money can make strong, myopic arguments regarding the 'here and now,' especially in America. The only 'counter' point to be made is through an underlying and undying FAITH.

Having faith: that is the stuff of the Divine anyway, is it not?

<u>NOTE</u>: I have chosen not to address that minority of people that I would classify as "SUB-Human" or, just pure evil. While angels on earth might be an exceptionally rare phenomenon not attracting very much attention, we certainly are all too painfully aware of the monstrous actions of a few people throughout history. These are the behaviors of savages even beneath the level of the most ferocious animals. While we know all about the Hitler's, the Stalin's, the Hannibal's, and the Pol Pot's of history, there is no need to revisit those well-worn accounts. Not when we have the same kind of behaviors still going on in contemporary times. Have we learned NOTHING at all from living?

I am specifically talking about the Middle East and actions by groups like Hamas and Israel's retaliations. It seems like "tit-for-tat" is a game that children play and not for a person in any Leadership position. Yet this is the only way that contemporary 'mangers' know how to act. The 'root' of the problem has been ignored, is currently ignored, and probably will always be ignored. Until the Westerners who created Israel without any understanding of the Muslim/Arab position, admit their colossal 'miscalculation' and create a permanently fair solution, this will never end. Of course, the cynics would argue that there is too much money to be made by the industrial/military complex to ever let the cost of innocent human lives deter their tremendous profit motives.

I guess the question becomes is there an inherent "violent" characteristic to Human Nature (just bubbling below the surface) that most strive to suppress, modify and/or control? Or do the 'blood merchants' tap into this quality in all of us to serve the bidding of our 'dormant' evil sides? To the 'purveyors' of this, there is a sliding scale for points of diminishing return upon various investment levels?

Are the Western Allies not resourceful enough to carve out enough land for each group to establish their own autonomy? Should not Israel have been created out of post-war Germany as reparations for the Holocaust? Why were the Palestinians punished for Germany's war crimes? Are the Allies not rich enough to spend the money to sufficiently incentivize each party to "get along" or suffer the consequences of total de-funding?

Finally, are pseudo-leader 'Allies' not powerful enough to bring about the threat of total 'destruction" if followers are non-compliant with world peace and harmony at risk? That has been the historical course of action for most non-leader types and the precedent that they follow anyway, is it not?

RE-TUNING THE "BELL CURVE"

If Management is seeing an unwed, pregnant teen and thinking:
"How Selfish?" then, Leadership is asking;
"What can I do to make sure she loves herself more?"

I happen to be a big believer in the normal distribution of the Bell Curve. You know, an 80%/20% rule suggesting that, approximately 80% of anything ('under' the "Bell") is where absolutely EVERYTHING is most appropriate (I.e., humanly "healthy") to exist yet, where only 20% of the world truly exists. Conversely, 80% of people actually live under the 'dangerously' worldly tails of 20% (10% at each extreme end of the curve). This is what I call the "UN-well" Curve (an upside-down Bell). This has certainly been my experience in both my professional and personal life. I do think it is about time, however, to bring the Bell Curve up to date by shedding some modern 'light' on it and maybe to 'tweak' it just a tad. While its simplicity had accounted for much of its appeal, I do not think that it will tarnish its image, reputation, or storied history too very much with a little bit of new interpretation and modification. This seems primarily needed due to evolution of individuals and institutions of this world as it presently exists.

In a world where most people think that "bigger is better" and 'more' is always preferable to 'less,' the strivings of individuals and organizations throughout history may have needed a sort of tunnel-vision in order to generate the remarkable progress that Humankind has accomplished. I think that the time has come to take off those 'blinders' and maybe re-assess when, enough-is-enough already, because many of us are choking on too much and we need to pay more attention to the far "tail" of that renown Bell Curve. I happen to see a significant similarity (problem) between the lowest 10% of that curve and the highest 10%. Under the middle 80% of that 'bell' is where the vast majority of people and institutions should be able to find their ideal "sweet spot" for every dimension of their existence. For individuals, it would best for the harmonious balance of their Physical, Intellectual, Emotional and Spiritual aspects. For organizations, it would be the same balance for their Goals, Power, Needs, and Culture.

The Bell Curve is very symmetrical and therein lies the secret of its appeal to me, its "balance." This can become a visual metaphor for how individuals should strive to live, create the most life 'leverage' from ones' own particular level of optimum balance. Is that not the only way in which a 120-pound person can toss a 200-pound person to the mat in a judo class? Is that not how a 150-pound person can hit a golf ball 325 yards? My hypothesis here is that a similar balance in ones' holistic life can produce equally impressive results in most areas of said life.

First, let me say a little more about the 'dangers' of an imbalanced life. Despite the theory that, "one can never be too rich or too thin," those messages usually come from the selling of outside, 'worldly' sources plying its own "trade" and/or grinding its own 'axe.' I believe the extreme top and the extreme bottom of every measure suffer terribly similar fates. Being too rich causes just as many difficulties as being too poor; just ask any working-person lottery winner? Being too smart can cause just as many difficulties as being too 'stupid;' just ask any "genius" who struggles to be understood? Complaining about being too short; talk to a 7-footer who cannot fit in anything 'conventional'? How about the struggles of the obese; try spending a week with anorexia/bulimia? Going too slow on the highways can cause just as many accidents as going too fast. While it may have been frustrating to have only **4** televisions channels as a kid, I find it even MORE frustrating to have to choose among <u>400!</u> Are we not just as suspicious of the 'stranger' who appears "too" nice as one who appears to be NOT "nice" at all?

I think the point is well taken here; the grass always SEEMS greener elsewhere but is not necessarily so. My contention is that the powerful outside forces of the world benefit most when either extreme is promoted, and individuals take the 'bait' (and WHY so many of the people make choices which place them under the 20% extremes of the curve). Both diets and gluttony are heavily sold, and those companies are looking for the most customers and not really caring WHO consumes WHAT! It is <u>more</u> than just *caveat emptor;* each buyer has to more than beware, each must know both him/herself as well as ALL of the available 'options' well enough to decide how they can best 'balance' his/her life. Of course doing so requires all of the hard work that is quite natural for people to want to avoid.

If this sounds like it is an epic struggle between the individual and the rest of the world, you are correct, it is! To me, it makes David and Goliath look like a 'fair' fight. There has always been pressure to conform to the 'flavor' of the day but never more than now. When it was just informational influence from ones' family, village, community or even country, the pressure was more limited and travelled more slowly. As media has become faster, further-reaching, and more powerful, parents, teachers, pastors, coaches, journalists, and mentors (those serving as the 'buffers' between the individual and the world) have been at a serious disadvantage (versus say, social media) to help protect and instruct as to what might be considered each person's 'healthy' balance. For example, there has always been commentary on what makes for an "attractive" female figure. Whether "Rubenesque" roundness or "heroin chic" gauntness, the ideal seems to have bordered on one 'fad' extreme or the other. There is no problem if one naturally fits into a particular 'trendy' style, or even if it required ONLY a 10% gain or loss to qualify. The issue, as I see it, is not for the 'lucky' ones who are born to 'fit' perfectly for their generation's ideal values. I worry more for the person who does not fit/fit-in and goes to extremes (E.g., pills, starvation, surgery, comfort eating, etc.) to force herself into an unnatural category. You know, the wicked stepsister trying to force a size 9 foot into a size 6 glass slipper. Then, she gets spiteful and vindictive towards Cinderella when it does not fit!

The challenge for any of us has never been nor ever will be to capitalize on our strengths but rather, to overcome our "weaknesses." Just as any head coach will game-plan to take advantage of another team's flaws, the world has its sights on our individual 'soft spots.' So, while our tendency is to take the path of least resistance and play to our strong suit, that strategy will only get us so far and most importantly, usually defines the end of our growth and the beginning of out decline. By working on our weaknesses, however, we can slow the 'inevitable' and continue our Human development. Of course nobody likes to first acknowledge weaknesses, then confront them objectively (maybe with some help?) and finally actually do the HARD work to minimize them (or eliminate them entirely!). Like my family used to say, the "higher" you want to build any 'structure' totally depends on the depth of the foundation that you are willing to dig in order to support the above-ground edifice. No one ever wants to do the exhausting work of digging the basement, but everyone just wants to see the view from the cupula. Another thing my philosophical grandpa used to say, "when it comes to life (what has) bitter taste is better for you."

Let us take the four Human dimensions one at a time beginning with the Physical. Obviously, while the World tends to "Judge a Book by its Cover," people of any substance do not. Since physical appearance is the first thing any of us see of one another, first impressions are unavoidable. Both the person being judged, and the person judging are strongly influenced by the expectations placed upon everyone by society. While being aware of those external standards is no crime for the "judger," placing any credence in their opinion/judgment is how and when we start to go down a 'barren' path. First, for the "judged" in all of us, self-acceptance and self-love is the best place to start. Acknowledging that and understanding why, tall is preferable to short; thin is preferable to fat; right is preferable to left; light is preferable to dark; hair is preferable to bald, etc. is nothing more than a concept of rarity/scarcity. The fewer 'things' that there are (supply) the more they are wanted (demand) by the few people who define their life (and can afford them) by acquiring/possessing things (as well as people 'objects'). That is the only reason diamonds are recognized as more "precious" than rubies, sapphires, or emeralds…it is their scarcity and the 'richest' people who can afford it will drive up their respective prices. "Lab"-created diamonds provide a good example symptomatic of our current cultural dilemmas.

The secret to physicality is being the "best that one can be" considering the 'gifts' one is given at birth. There really is truly little that one can change from that anyway. It only takes about a week for everyone to realize whether a "blonde" is natural or not? Why not "lusterize" dark hair rather than dry it out? Does one not realize that, if one gets breast implants that one does NOT have big breasts, one just has silicone bags under her skin? I understand that there are tremendous cultural pressures to conform but that does not mean that it is healthy nor that it will not cause deep underlying and longer-term (psychological/emotional) problems. Things like mini-skirts, halter-tops, muscle shirts, stiletto heels and yoga pants only really look good on such a small factional segment of the population. The extraordinary burden falls on the rest of the population to realize what is really healthy/best/'right' for themselves. Then, make the conscientious choice NOT to wear anything that is unhealthy, unflattering, or downright "wrong" for THEM.

Once one has accepted one's appearance and has decided to love it (or at least like it a lot), the focus can be directed at enhancing the existing 'good' rather than some bad attempt at camouflaging the 'bad.' I am always amazed that, no matter how expensive (and good) a toupee, most everyone can always tell or at least hazard a guess (that cannot be healthy for any individual). When one decides to go with the 'shaved head' look instead, to me it exudes much more confidence outwardly and probably feels much more attractiveness inwardly. I guess this is a classic example of life giving someone 'lemons' and them making some delicious 'lemonade.' There is nothing wrong with looking the best one can look just not crossing over the 'line' that might define someone as artificial/unreal. In other words, fitting very nicely under the "normal' 80% section of the Bell Curve for ONESELF even though it might not be under the section that is reserved for the "majority" of what one DOES NOT possess.

Once we define our physical characteristics as healthy (best possible) for our own individuality, it becomes necessary to consider the next most important dimension of our Humanness. I am referring to the thing that most scientists consider the best Human advantage in the world, our large brain. Humans certainly would **<u>NOT</u>** win any tests of physicality (I.e., speed-cheetah, strength-elephant) or even 'beauty' (peacock, monarch butterfly) versus the best animals. We can out-think them, however, (unless A.I. renders us to "2nd" place on that) although animals would also 'win' most 'sensing' competitions. While I agree with the scientists of this assessment of Human brainpower, I do not think it is the most important facet to define our best Humanity (more on that later). The issue here is not that we are more rational/logical than anything in the animal kingdom but rather the fact that there are so many differences (E. g. creative, analytical, etc.) AMONG all of the eight types of Human (Multiple) Intelligences. This has been much of the work associated with left-brain versus right-brain dominance (E.g. "Emotional" intelligence-E.Q.). In the interest of knowing how each youngster stacks up in that area, we might provide much better direction on categories of K-12 curricula. Specifically, many benefits can be learned by the Myers-Briggs-type testing. Even the fortunate students usually discover where they fit into one of the 16 possible classifications after 18 years old which can be too late to <u>fully</u> benefit although, certainly better late than NEVER!

The authorities in the U.S. certainly (and most of the Western World) historically limit the value of Human Intelligence to only two forms: words/language ("readin,' writin'") and numbers ("rithmetic.") While these SAT-type measures certainly reinforce the WASPy and chauvinistic narrative, it is a severe limitation and underrepresentation of the concept of Multiple Intelligences (E. g's. "Nature," "Spiritual," "Personal," "Kinesthetic," "Music"). As the Culture becomes ever more diverse, the arrogance/narrowness of this thinking becomes not only undervaluing but downright untenable. As is the case with most of these self-serving criteria, many worthwhile intellectual contributions are left out of the mix, thereby limiting the success of the 'overall' for the gratification of the few (WASP influenced Educational Test Service). I guess the problem starts with education's administrators everywhere and on every level, who want to make things 'easy' on themselves and their Trustee/Government constituents. If not, would not high school hours be more like 10:00am – 5:00pm in order to maximize the natural biological learning 'clocks' of adolescents?

The classic example of this is Human "creativity" much of which is 'flushed' out of students in an effort to streamline the boundaries (lowest common denominators) of classroom lessons and behavior. Much of creativity withers away if allowed to lay fallow until college age. In a country (and maybe World?) where Economics is the business of each day, it has been extremely hard for anyone who has a 'different' Intelligence to thrive. I am encouraged by the gradual transformation from an I.Q. world to an E.Q, (Emotional Intelligent) evaluation. To paraphrase a great book title, my advice to everyone would be: "Define your own Intelligence in order to DO what YOU Love…and…then, the Money will Follow."

While Intelligence may separate us from the animal kingdom, I think our Emotional component enables us to better connect with our greater planetary life. While it is definitely best to avoid both Emotional extremes, there is a tremendous range of heathy and acceptable feelings under the "Bell." Things like differences in Human "sensitivity" and psychological "disposition" provide for a rich, and diverse 'palette' from which to paint the total Human experience. The World would have us limit the range of our Emotions to a prescribed and narrow/shallow scope. Only the incredibly young and old can afford to be honest: men should not cry; women should not be assertive; blah, blah, blah! If that is written anywhere, I would like to demand a RE-write/RE-submit. The World is looking for sheep who will follow some unjustified (slaughtered) convention and specifically, the 'white' sheep whose wool will bring the most money at market. If one is born a "black cat" (mixed metaphor intended) instead, the World will make up unfounded 'superstitions' to get you to change and if you do not, will ostracize you from the rest of their NORMAL Emotionally constituted folks. What a crock!

I was blessed with a, wise-beyond-our-years friend who once told me: "Just be yourself!" I confess that I did not understand the full import of that advice at the time, although I never forgot it and harkened back to it often on the long journey to becoming "myself." At that time (like 10th grade) I was desperately trying to fit it to the "normal" teenage cliques. It was obvious to my friend that I was trying TOO hard. Many of the cliques back then may have seemed 'popular' (common) but for my psychological framework and emotional orientation, they were too extreme (E.g., "jocks," "punks," etc.) It was not until the gradual climb unto becoming the real ME that I understood myself and accepted my position under the Bell. It was pretty far left but underneath it, nonetheless. Being called a "contrarian" or thinking "androgynously" or having a "immature" spirit or acting "entrepreneurially" was much easier to eventually accept than continually trying to fit a label that, was NOT bad at all, it just was **not** for me. So the simple message and lesson here is ones' Emotional life will never be particularly good until/unless it is one's OWN-genuine, authentic, and sincere to the person involved, regardless of what ANYONE thinks.

So, if Emotional health and balance helps up feel good about our place in an un-balanced and mostly un-healthy world, what role should our individual "Spiritual" side play in our 'quest' to exist under the "Bell"? Feeling good about our 'connection' with the timeless and spaceless universe, I think. Of course, organized religion can create the exact same type and amount of pressure to conform spiritually that the fashion industry does about our bodies. The educational system might confound our minds in the way that multi-media (more than ever with 'social") does the same our hearts. Listen, I fully understand that trainers can help us with our own physical fitness, tutors can help us with difficult academic subjects and counselors can help us deal better with our emotions so, "clergy" can certainly help us with any struggles of faith. We have become too dependent upon the so called, "experts" when their help should be reserved for only the most difficult situations and <u>not</u> just 'everyday' living. Like Bob Dylan sang: "We don't need a weatherman to tell which way the wind blows." The problem I have with any of these 'helpers' (especially with our soul) is that I do not believe INDIVIDUALS respond best to the external 'advice' (maybe if it were called "ad-VIRTUE"?) necessary for viable economic effectiveness and time efficiencies. More than any of these four Human aspects, our spiritual journey is the MOST specific/particular and the one which supports the best individual "Full-Potential," R.O.I. (Return on Investment), that is to say, OUR OWN peace, love, and happiness.

Like the other three aspects, the World of religious influence seems to live and work outside of standard deviations. From the zealous fanatic, over on the right tail, who eats, drinks, and breathes dogma to the dyed-in-the-wool atheist (Left Tail) who applies his/her: "I'm from Missouri…SHOW ME" decisive test to each area of faith. The acts of healthy balance/common sense beliefs seem UN-able to coexist under the Bell. This uninhabitability seems to play havoc with all but the few conceivers of ample imagination and vision. In a world where both literal interpretation of the Bible and pure Darwinism draws the most diametrically opposed followers, why are not there more devotees of the explanation for life as: ***Divinely Designed with Ample Free Choices and No Specific Results Planned?*** ("intelligent design"). That has appealed to me because it allows for plenty of room for specific beliefs without reliance upon exacting unprovable details. And yes, I think all believers would fall under the normal 80% which exists under the Bell. It might cripple "tithing" but certainly allow each person to balance his/her own level of cynicism and hope.

It certainly sounds difficult enough to find ones' normal place under the Bell for each individual aspect (Physical; Intellectual; Emotional; Spiritual) of his/her own uniqueness. For example, I knew conclusively that I could not become a professional football/basketball player by 15 years old. I did not know for certain that I could not be a professional baseball player until I was 18 years old. My dreams for professional golfing died at 22 years of age (but I remain the "Happy Hacker"). My ability to be an active, fit, and healthy Physical being still lives on and I have my sights firmly set on becoming a professional Centenarian. Not too bad acceptance and revised, resubmitted plan, huh?

I was blessed with quick wit and a good memory, and I thought that the best use of these gifts was to make beaucoup bucks in corporate America. It did not hurt those assumptions that I grew up in the working class ("tweener") or that the World was very supported of my using my 'talents' to make money for everyone involved (I got a lot of "atta boyz"). Much like prostitution is about sex and not about love (no judgment here; a noble profession that should be legalized), corporate business is about profits and not necessarily about personal satisfaction. So, after a well-earned mid-life crisis, I was lucky enough to drop out of the work-a-day corporate reality enough to return to school to become a professor. I swapped empty analysis for hungering creativity and was able to **give back** instead of merely **giving out** and did not have to **give up**. I am pretty proud of myself for this transformation to a life "passion" but am also grateful for having had much help along the way.

Emotionally, I was miscast, and misfit within the upwardly mobile materialistic world. Again, nothing wrong with that, simply wrong for me. At that time, Italian-Americans were classified as the "least assimilated" of the immigrant ethnicities. Emotions truly had little place into WASPy corporate culture. For Italians, it has always been about *"La Via de la Familia"* and the business honchos do not really care if you have to choose work over family and so, for a long time, I went along with that. My Emotional immaturity caused a clueless understanding of love so, I ruined some really good potential relationships along the way (in addition to a well-earned ulcer). Much like my Physical limitation realizations and my Intellectual calling, I continued to be the poster boy for "Better Late than Never." I finally did get my own family after switching to the academic life where I had the time to **<u>not</u>** have to make that ('Sophies' Choice') between meetings and dance recitals or client entertainment and soccer games. Whew!

No one knows when the spiritual journey ends so, I do not know how far I have left to go? I do realize, however, accepting my modest Physical abilities, working towards my Intellectual 'calling' of teaching and having my three children all have contributed greatly to my Emotional 'availability" for better Human Development. These have all been a true and total blessing. As a 'recovering' Catholic, I had to go far afield to reconcile the discrepancies between what worked and what did not work for ME in MY life. I am sure my Catechism teachers are *"verklempt"* but seeing Spiritual explanations above-and-beyond the need for just faith/hope/charity in order to be of useful reality and not strictly be about guilt and blame helped a lot. God so loved the world that, he chose more than just a 'handful' of his creations on the Third Stone from the Sun to be considered "HIS" <u>worthwhile</u> people.

As I said, it is only **difficult** (long and exhausting internal work) to find our own place under the Bell for each of the four dimensions to our life. The <u>impossibility</u> of coordinating each of those four places among themselves, as the saying goes, will take a little longer and be the hardest work ever. In other words, choosing between going to the gym and reading a book is not an easy choice at all. No matter where you placed yourself in each of these categories, it will always be an "apples & oranges" comparison (I.e., "relative balance"). Not for the "hulk" or the "bookworm" but remember, those extremes are to be avoided at all balancing costs. The toughest choices are those among varying shades of gray.

In my opinion, the greatest gift of all from the "Divine" is the gift of "Relativity." Since our own "Perception is **our own** Reality," if one has enough internal security/strength, no external source should be able to disrupt ones' own sense of truth, beauty, love, happiness, intelligence or any other of one's values. There has been too much emphasis on the **one & only** BEST for anything and/or anyone. When in actual reality, things really work "best" when <u>each</u> Parent thinks her/his Child is **best** and <u>every</u> Child thinks his/her Parents are **best**. When a man believes that HIS wife is the most beautiful and a wife believes HER husband is the most handsome. Likewise, due to the Theory of Relativity, one person might feel "blessed" for their $50,000 a year salary while another might feel 'lacking' with a salary of $500,000 per year. Any objective reality check supplies no beneficial answers in these cases. Can you deny the genuine level of pure joy of a "Special Olympian" who breaks his/her record of a personal best performance even though that accomplishment might be nowhere close to an actual "World's Record"? This, while the "Regular Olympian" is distraught over a fourth-place finish, one hundredth of a second behind the "gold." It is ALL Relative just as the world has ALL Relative-S!

The favorite example I have about my own balancing 'act' is about my Intellect and my Emotions. As said, I was blessed with quick wit and an ability to make people laugh sometimes. At a younger age, I thought that creatively using my brain for humor was of the highest order utility. I am sure that many times (both knowingly and unknowingly) I got laughs at the expense of other people' hurt feelings. I have since learned that using that same creative Intelligence to say a kind word or to turn someone's frown upside down is even more rewarding and satisfying that a cheap (although witty) laugh. Here is the big secret trick, ready for it? By combining Intellectual acumen with Emotional sensitivity used through Physical ability, you get Spiritual Enlightenment which, feels the absolute best of all! It was hard for me to change and a big risk in giving up the comedian-in-me though. I had a long, successful history of scoring great 'points' being funny and to be willing risk ALL that (yikes!) in order to be considered "nice"? What I did not realize then is that getting laughs is extrinsic, so it seems more valuable to the World but being "nice" is of more intrinsic value which is synergistic and cumulative. Without that (invisible to most) process, there is extraordinarily little chance of gaining one iota of one's own ultimate Human balance or 'parking' anywhere near one's "sweet spot" under the Bell. The ONLY parking place where one does NOT get a 'ticket' for a living violation!

R.O.I.–AL TREATMENT

If Management is making YOUR 'best' dish for dinner guests then,
Leadership is learning to make THEIR 'favorite' dish.

It is common to refer to the concept of "Return on Investment" when considering Business and/or Financial ventures. Quite simply, "how much money can I expect to get BACK for the amount that I GIVE"? Usually this is expressed in terms of an Annual percentage of the Total. For example, if one invests $1,000 in a 5-year-Bond and at the end of five years receives $1,500 back, a **simple** (not compound) R.O.I. would be expressed as a, "10% Return Annually over 5 years totaling 50% for my initial Investment".

With the cultural trend of People viewing themselves as 'Products' to be "Branded," I was thinking that it might be important to offer up potential Human R.O.I.'s to be evaluated and considered in light of all of the options available. Most everyone works to have money and they have a multitude of choice combinations of what, how, when, where, and why to spend his/her dollars. Even the terms "disposable" and "discretionary" are of themselves very subjectively defined by each individual. For example, one person might define cosmetics as "essential," another as a "luxury" and yet another as a "complete waste."

I can see three (3) major investment categories which might produce significantly different R.O.I.'s. Within each major category, we can consider two (2) different sub-classifications. As follows:

BEST Returns on Investment

HEALTH-

When my Mother used to say, "if you have your Health, you have everything," I used to think "yeah that's what you say when you have NOTHING else." Now I understand that she was very correct and wise in her belief. I also remember reading an *Interview with God* where, among other things, God wondered why people "spent all of their Health gaining money and then spent all of their money to gain <u>back</u> their Health?" Not unlike the message of a Mexican story I once read where a man worked like a maniac all his life so he could "enjoy himself" (to go fishing) when he (healthfully) retired while criticizing a man who spent his life (healthfully) fishing (as a 'job') to "enjoy himself" and NOT working like a maniac!

The lessons here seem pretty much the same, I.e., short-term solutions do not pay the highest Return on Investment and they might actually obscure the better R.O.I. which is based on a longer-term period. With Human Nature being what it is, most of us find it almost impossible to delay/defer gratification/payment even if our 'brain' understands the benefit of doing so. Quite simple, we just do not want to have to wait for whatever life satisfaction is possible and continue to live by the fallacy that "a bird in the hand is worth two in the bush." While maybe true for hunting, I do not believe that is true as far as individual health is concerned.

Most of us want guarantees up-front for the time/money/effort we invest and do not have the faith to wait for a "return" on our payout. So, it does not seem to make sense to spend extra time/money eating healthy and taking 'vitamins' when high sugar/salt/fat (FAST food) tastes good NOW! It does not seem logical to us to leave a fun party early, in order to get the necessary healthy sleep when one can "sleep when one is dead." Nor does it seem rational to invest all of the necessary energy to exercise today when one might die in an "accident" before reaching "old age." In all these cases, it takes a tremendous amount of faith in the future to override our intellectual assessment of the here and now. At the least, a very personal decision has to be made. Hell, many people do better preventative maintenance on their automobiles than on their bodies…including mental health care here as well!

There seems nothing more gratifying than living a healthy, pain free and active life to a ripe, old age. Conversely, nothing seems more tragic than a highly medicated, immobile, and unaware-of-one's surroundings senior citizen softly knocking at death's door for any length of time before 80.

Individuals are certainly not alone in these choices; there has been more help along the way. For example, governments have periodically stepped in where and when the common good of "society" is concerned. Laws have been enacted to eliminate tobacco advertising for example. Quite often this legislation is usually too little and too late (thanks to uber powerful tobacco lobby) and NOT before tremendous costs of Human life and material property (although many people <u>still</u> smoke). People on a "mission" have prompted causes to evolve into legislation like Mothers Against Drunk Driving (MADD) (although many people <u>still</u> drive while "buzzed"). Apparently, there has not yet been enough tragedy yet to warrant Anyone Against Texting While Driving (AATWD?). We certainly have many more "public health" resources than in year's past, but the debate still rages on about 'healthcare' being a "civil right or a privilege" and to what degree? Does a 60-year-old 'deserve' a hip replacement but an 80-year-old ONLY a "walker"? It depends on whether it is MY father or not! Even further, should we <u>limit</u> trauma care expenditures to a motorcycle rider who does NOT wear a helmet and/or charge more for health insurance if one is OBESE?

Likewise, Individuals have access to much more information than ever before in history, but does that clarify or confuse? Consumer activists have certainly gotten things like product/ingredient labeling on packaging. Technology has given most people access to reviews and ratings of virtually every product/service out there. One still has to be motivated enough to' 'research' the alternatives, capable of comprehending what might be intentionally/unintentionally complicated and then take the time/money/energy to navigate through their complex 'findings.' So, in "theory," individuals CAN take more responsibility for their own Health, but the "practice" is for most people to opt for the path of least resistance. This leads to their own, short-term solution rather than to become so easily overwhelmed. Most recently the 'debate' on pandemic vaccinations for Covid being "mandatory' for: EITHER the common good OR a violation of one's control over individual body rights? And just think, one previous ("greatest") generation volunteered to fight the Nazis way over in Europe. Is a vaccine asking more or less of citizens than that? Conversely, have Big Pharma and Big Government been completely forthcoming about all of the risks? I guess the Supreme Court will first have to hear a case called "Doe vs. Dive" in order to challenge it 50 years from now.

EDUCATION/EXPERIENCE-

Another "best" Return on Investment is in the area of formal Education (and equivalent Learned-from-Life experience like travel) but like Health, its 'payoff' usually must be realized (delayed) over the longer term. We have all heard the estimate that College Graduates make a million dollars MORE than non-graduates over the course of an earnings' lifetime. That may or may not change in the future, but I think it is safe to say that, each year of additional "higher" education translates to more earning 'potential.' BUT, as with Healthcare, one has to pay in the 'present' with time, energy, and a lot of money up-front for the possibility of payoffs deferred and realized/ recognized gradually over the course of time.

Aside from the money potential, most would agree that education positively impacts the QUALITY of Human life as well. This seems true whether measured as "knowledge for its own sake/reward" or the potential for more happiness, health, understanding, appreciation, self-sufficiency, and better mental health. History has seemed to have borne out that education can equal more 'smarts' which can lead to more power, prestige, health, status, leadership, healthier relationships, etc. At the very least, people with "formal" Education as well as 'useful' Lessons Learned-from-Life Experience seem to have better potential for both surviving and thriving against whatever the World might present.

While it takes much discipline, dedication, and determination to invest in a future payout, much of the return "rewards" are uniquely individual in nature and therefore, despite any demographic analysis, each person must decide and define for themselves the exact nature of their "investment." For example, ANY major discipline of study as well as a specific subject matter have much different 'value' (subjective) depending on the particular person doing the studying. One person might feel that a Business degree is NOT worth any greater career salary gained while another person might believe a Fine Arts degree is the best possible use of tuition money despite slimmer job prospects. Even more relevant these days might be the renewed interest (especially from white males) in the more technical/mechanical trades in lieu of a bachelor's degree. "To EACH his/her own," I guess?

BREAKEVEN Returns on Investment

REAL ESTATE

Like the name implies this investment is "real" in that it has always been something 'tangible' (land) that can at least "hold" its value and keep up with "inflation" and/or other measures of increased cost of living. Owning one's home was pretty much a thing for the wealthy until the "American Dream" came onto the World scene. The fact that many working/middle classes families got 'rich' just through home ownership in the 20th century will probably turn out to be an anomaly 'blip' on historical records. It has certainly been better, however, than paying rent but in the future, it might prove to be little more than a 'placeholder' in which to just keep up with perpetually rising costs (I.e., CPI).

More than a pure wealth creator, home ownership is probably a better investment for non-financial indicators. You know a "house does not make it a home," etc. The qualitative and intangible benefits are probably the best reasons for investing in Real Estate that is "lived" in by the owners. I would even include second/vacation homes in this assessment. Things like pride of ownership, sense of community belonging, and family cohesiveness truly make sense for a return on Human "needs/wants" for the price of the real estate. Obviously, there is a very wide disparity among all of the neighborhoods ("location, location, location") expenses in which homes can be purchased but this concept falls under the "rising tide lifts ALL boats" principle.

Speculative real estate and other 'Collectables' are only worth what someone else is willing to pay the owner. If one looks at the big-picture, long-term 'bottom line,' there are winners and losers along the way and at best, I will hazard to say that these activities (overall) probably just keep pace with the costs of living (inflation). I think they do represent a pleasurable activity for the group of people (E.g., traders, brokers, flippers, churners) who 'play' in this arena. I do concede there is value in the "buying and selling" features of these pursuits and my assumption is the vast majority of players CAN afford to win or lose and they are NOT playing with their 'meal' money. Although I am sure there are the normal percentage of "addicted" types who can NOT control getting themselves into financial 'trouble' at times.

FINANCIAL INSTRUMENTS

This category would include the Equity and Debt 'vehicles' that are used to derive better returns than saving's account interest or money under the mattress. We all hear the stories of people who allegedly hit the 'lottery' by purchasing an "Apple" or "Amazon" at issue but those are mostly "folklore" that get magnified way out of proportion (**everyone** was at Woodstock). Mostly, there are winners and losers who over time and across the 'board' are barely staying ahead of inflation. This includes the "experts" who make their living on "Wall Street," the Mutual Funds aggregates and all of the "Indexes." So, by all means, participation is better than NOT participating but just like "treading water" is better than drowning, BUT you never really get **that far** ahead. I might also include other things like "investment grade" art, antiques, precious metals, etc. in this category. It mostly seems like a "zero sum" (factoring for inflation) 'balancing' out game to me in that the gainers equal the losers.

WORST Returns on Investment

MOTORIZED LAND VEHICLES, WATERCRAFT, AND OTHER BOY 'TOYS'

This category is filled with products which depreciate rapidly and deeply. The question that everyone needs to ask themselves is: "Can I afford the <u>depreciation</u>?" In some cases, like basic transportation, a motorized vehicle may be more of a 'necessity' than a 'luxury' but in those cases, the secret is buying for function that matches one's budget. Overspending on products (for image, status, prestige, exclusivity, etc.) that one cannot afford is an effective way to get a really **bad** Return on one's Investment. I see two noticeably big issues here that ironically, are inexorably linked together. The first one is Human Nature's Ego. At the risk of sounding politically incorrect, I would even go so far as to hazard the stereotype that, these mostly stem from the MALE ego (I.e., one is only as 'sexy' as one's car). The second is that in a competitive, capitalistic, and free-market economy, the world of business' job is to inflate the importance of material possessions through tempting our emotional weaknesses and psychological insecurities. This is most certainly done for the purpose of its own Financial gain. The World can easily accomplish this by using all of its considerable psychological/sociological marketing resources to turn Human Ego WANTS into Human Ego NEEDS.

"BLING" AND DECOR

Do not feel left out ladies, we have many bad investments for you as well. I classify these as Fashion, Fads, Furnishings, and other general Body Adornments/'Adjustments.' The same way that the World has convinced Men that, their self-worth is tied into things one possesses like the car they drive (representative of the money one has), the World has convinced Women that their self-worth is tied into how they look on the 'outside.' Both of these may work IF one's wealth can afford it but when one buys these things (E.g., cosmetic surgery; obsession with "Nails") and they CANNOT afford them, then the downward 'slide' to negative Return on

Investment begins (starting with unmanageable debt). Let us not forget the need to continually re-decorate out homes with the latest 'furnishings'. Advertisers and credit card companies are more than willing to facilitate this downward slide because the rest of us pay for any unpaid debt via 'higher' interest charges. Unless we are talking about "museum quality" jewelry, there is much more "sentimental" value to these investments than the "liquidation" value of these compared to the original purchased price.

"DANGER WILL ROBINSON"

Hopefully, it is obvious that ANY kind of Gambling (including lottery tickets) is absolutely the worst kind of investment to make since the odds are ALWAYS in favor of the 'house'!

BOTTOM LINE

So, life is a tug-of-war between our own Human Nature living in the World and our higher ("divine") consciousness. And, if it feels like having each of our arms tied to a different draft horse pulling in opposite directions, that is because it is. The World is shrewd enough to pull hard on one arm (with temptations) in order to appeal to our Ego. While the other arm seems to pull 'less hard' with our financial limitations and Super Ego. Only the strongest of us can resist the strength of that force. It is just like the perennial "angel" on one shoulder and the "devil" on the other, each whispering in one ear cross talking to our brain (conscience) in order to convince us of each 'argument.' Whether one describes our 'referee' as our conscience, our Super-Ego, our morality, or any other concept, this is a veritable 'David' versus the 'Goliath' of the world/ego/'sins.' It is becoming a harder and harder 'battle' for individuals' 'sensibility' to win. It will help, however, to make the choices/decisions which provide the BEST Returns on ALL of your Investments.

THE NEW READIN,'
RIGHTIN' & 'RITHMETIC

If Management is seeing a poor, old man smoking and thinking,
"How Stupid?" then, Leadership is compassionately asking:
"Why Is this the ONLY Pleasure he has left in his life?"

I may be feeling nostalgic or plain old, but it seems to me like we need a revised slogan for what is essential for children (of all ages) to learn in life's schools. The world has, fairly-recently, evolved to the point where, technological advances (god, I hate Apple "spell") can pretty much do all of our Reading and Writing through various voice-recognition computer software applications. On the other hand, we have been losing the need for any kind of Mathematics since calculators have become affordable in the "pocket" variety. Maybe that is actually a blessing in disguise? Haven't students always hated that 'stuff' anyways?

Well, people should get ready to miss the "good ole days" since they will learn to hate the new academic mandates even more and guess what? The new imperatives are even harder to master than the 3, "R's". I am talking about what many refer to as the "soft skills" of people Leadership. You see, most of the old school 'hard' skills of Management can be almost completely handled by technology and therefore, "Leadership has become the 'new' Management." Aside from a few learning institutions, I am not really sure that any curricula has caught 'up' or even caught 'on' with what people of the 21st century are REALLY going to need to know in order to thrive and maybe just to survive.

It seems to me that the old disciplines of planning, organizing, deciding, assessing, analyzing, evaluating and most of all, controlling are being done for us by the purveyors of our life choices and their mega data resources. The need for change these days is even moving faster than the perpetual "new" math and the uncertainty of circumstances happening to us has become even less predictable than whether Pluto is a planet or a Mouse-ka-dog? So, aside from getting rich from inane actions and insane thoughts, by "subscribing" to some YouTube channel, one is able to buy all of the knowledge one needs. What can one study-to-learn in order to prepare oneself against obsolescence and one's eventual DNA extinction?

Since none of us can anticipate the 'macro' events that might happen to us, I am suggesting that we begin to equip people with more of the tools necessary to control a fighting chance for their survival. I am thinking that contacting each individual's own personal creativity ability is a good place to start. I am not talking about artistic talent here but every person's ability to generate alternative solutions to the inevitable problems which beset all of us on a regular basis. We all have enough creativity to innovate for our own individual circumstances although I am not suggesting that we all have <u>equal</u> amounts of creativity, just <u>equitable</u> amounts. Just like, for all intents and purposes, a 250-pound person has the arm muscle mass to do a pullup while a 150-pound person should have much less total arm muscle but relatively, probably enough to pull up his or her own 150 pounds.

More specifically, I am talking about the obtuse, harder-to-quantify/define concepts of **Flexibility, Versatility, Adjustability, Adaptability,** and the overall Human **Variable Agility Ability** that will be of crucial importance to each person's ability to deal with life in the future. While I certainly do not pretend to have any curriculum for each of these, let us at least take them one-at-time to better explain what they are, what they might include and how they might be different.

In no particular order:

<u>FLEXIBILITY-</u>

The flipside of an on-time/on-demand world is that people get so used to (and believe, entitled to) having absolutely EVERYTHING their own particular, individual way and therefore they have a difficult time accepting substitutes or dare I say, even "second best" on anything. There is a danger in demanding or even expecting extremely specific outcomes from such a random world. Sheryl Crow said a wise thing when she sang "wanting what you have instead of having what you want." The entire American conspicuous consumption 'machine' runs by turning "wants" into "needs" for the hordes of ravenous customers and their personal appetites. (Not to 'pick' on Apple but isn't their motto something like: "WE invent products that people don't know they've got-to-have yet?"). If no one thought there was any product and/or service "to die for," maybe genuine needs and 'optional' wants would be in more of a healthy perspective and realistic proportion?

Having been taught that wasting food is a "sin," my most diametrically opposed experience of total IN-Flexibility happened when walking into a friend's house for the first time. There upon the kitchen counter were 3, two-liter bottles of soda, each about half empty. The 'brands' were 7-Up, Sierra Mist and Sprite. Apparently, this family was so discriminating that they could not even agree on any **one** lemon-lime/non-diet flavor soda at a time. The marketing person in me wanted to conduct a "double-blind" taste test to prove my hypothesis that this was totally self-indulgent behavior by three, NON-Flexible entitle-ees (I.e., they really could not tell the difference without brand labels.) I am pretty certain that before entirely consumed, much of the product went 'flat' and was thrown out. I guess wasting food and adding to environmental clutter must make some people feel very deservingly special, indeed.

The great 'trick' here is that the purveyors of our HEART'S DESIRES are in a vicious competition with each other to turn them into NEEDS (and selling MORE product whether wasted or not). If we could learn to like any cola, instead of a specific brand; or any light beer regardless of its graphic can design; or any number of athletic shoe options, we would gain much power and control over the sellers. I think everyone can relate to the fast-food burger wars and I like that example. When people ask me my favorite fast food, I reply "discounted fast food." After all, isn't a burger just a burger? Like my Dad used to say: "yes, it is true that, no two snowflakes are exactly alike but who the hell cares, I've got to shovel the whole driveway." The truth is that I am FLEXIBLE enough to appreciate the slight difference between each fast-food burger but not so 'hypnotized' as to which one I absolutely have to have at any given time. I appreciate the diversity and somehow think I **beat** the companies (by giving them less money and keeping more of it for myself) if I am willing to eat the Whopper, Big Mac, Wendy's Single, or Thickburger depending on who is offering the <u>best deal (coupons?)</u>. I am not suggesting that I, or anyone, should eat something they do **not** like, but rather, having the ability to genuinely **like (and appreciate)** DIFFERENT things and to place value on that (rare) ability. Much like a guitar player who is equally comfortable with a Gibson, a Fender or a Martin might be able to "sit in" with more bands than a player who only can, or is only willing, to play only one brand. This FLEXIBILITY also helps keep the 'peace' with whomever I am 'negotiating' with who might have narrower choice preferences and/or a more limited selection acceptance. I. e. I will eat ANY burger that someone else absolutely HAS to have.

<u>VERSTAILITY-</u>

How might "Versatility" be different from the above-mentioned "Flexibility." Using the guitar example, a player who can play a jazzy-funk style, a country-rock style and a folksy-pop style might have a better chance of working more than someone who can only play one style. As times get tougher and money gets tighter, the Versatile person should have a much better chance to survive than a more limited 'player.' Conversely, when things are 'good,' Versatility would net more opportunities for the Versatile 'players' to thrive vis-à-vis the non-Versatile ones. The same could be said for an athlete who can play more than only one position and the teacher who can perform equally well on more than only one subject area.

It seems in the last 50 years or so, society has really come to emphasize and reward "specialization" thereby narrowing life's focus more are more. As information has exploded, that specialization has become necessary as the time we have available each day has NOT increased (beyond 24/7/365) to meet the information demand. Nor have our I.Q.'s kept up anywhere the near pace of the collective computerized mega data memory/storage/ speed capacities. If truth be told, the cycle has gone from "generalized broad" knowledge to "specialized deep" knowledge before arriving at the current demand for BOTH broad and deep knowledge/ability/talent/skill from any professional hoping to compete at an important level. Just like it used to be that football backs were "fast" while linemen were "strong;" now runners and blockers must be BOTH fast AND strong in order to be able to compete for a paycheck….no exceptions! Just compare the number of things that musical entertainers must do today as compared to those of previous generations. Frank Sinatra just had to be "cool," and Elvis just needed to be "hot." Today, one needs to be able to write music and lyrics, play multiple instruments, sing great, act in their performances, dance in their videos as well as having to 'model' for their ads and PR. Taylor Swift is more of a C.E.O. than a chanteuse. All of the collective 'bars' have been raised all across all of our cultural institutions.

ADJUSTABILITY-

Whether it be an author continually rewriting drafts or sailors continuously trimming a boat's sails, the best never rests easy upon the *status quo*. As they say, something is already out of date as soon as its ink dries. Does that suck? Sure! Why? Because it is Human Nature to dislike and resist change. There is a natural tendency to be lazy towards things they are not "broke." The problem is that things are **not** optimal long before they are classified as "broken" (i-Phones?). Even when they do break, it seems easier for most to replace or do a major "fix" rather than preventing/maintaining (patching elbows and knees) along the way with minor and gradual "fixes." Looking at clothes, for example, it used to be quite common to repair (anyone been to a "shoemaker" lately?) high-quality items for longer life rather than replacing cheaper items with an ever-greater quantity of equally faster-wearing-out items. When did we start to think that we need so many more items that we can possibly use? Hell, most people will not even maintain Health on a gradual basis but prefer to deal with built-up 'catastrophes' with major surgery and/or radical medications. It may be just correlation and not causation, but the "happiest" people are earth live in Scandinavia and the Norwegians/Fins/Danes/Swedes have much fewer personal possessions per capita than the United States. It is much harder to care for and maintain wearables than to abuse and discard them, but the vast majority of consumers seem to prefer the latter, whether or not they can afford to do so, whether it makes them happy or not?

I guess the first and most major step of "Adjustability" is to be able to recognize the legitimate need for something or <u>not</u>. Many accidents are caused by "over-correcting" an Adjustment or Adjusting unnecessarily. Sounds like a good lesson for Adjusting 101, since, as much as it may be needed, I do not think it comes naturally to most people (just like Geometry does not). Even though the act of selling or donating ones' seldom worn, good condition clothes is a better-than-nothing choice, there are much better alternatives. Assuming that one cannot 'beat' the manipulative and pernicious nature of the fashion industry (or the Healthcare industry), at least the wise person can 'compete' by raising a hemline or combining 'accent' accessories to "Adjust' their current wardrobe rather than "throw out the baby with the bathwater." Going back to our author example at the beginning of this section, which is precisely what is done with revised textbooks; they are called "new" Editions. They are hardly new at all but merely ADJUSTMENTS to the original work. Sailors Adjust to changes in wind direction by understanding the consequences of any potential subtle Adjustment (Racecar Drivers?) and by anticipating it before it happens. So do the best golfers and hockey players, by the way. Seems like a lot of important usefulness for everyday life ability.

ADAPTABILITY-

Dinosaurs are way cool, and cockroaches are disgusting right? I am not saying it is better to be an existing roach rather than an extinct dino, but the real question is: how best to survive anything (cockroaches can and will eat ANYTHING) that comes their way? The answer obviously is being to be able to "Adapt" to ever-changing environments, conditions, and situations. While it might have taken millions of years or one catastrophic event to rid the world of T-Rex and 'friends,' most likely it will only take a couple generations and a few much smaller events to relegate one's DNA to encased-in-amber status. While our entire species might be subject to environmental catastrophes (E.g., pandemic), as individuals we must focus on the things that are more likely to slowly but surely and painfully usher about our demise. Things like career/jobs; geographic location options; lifestyle choices; and relationship alternatives offer critical areas for potential Adaptability or not.

For example, failing to Adapt to changing technologies (E. g. A.rtificial I.ntelligence) will be a significant liability in one's ability to find and keep quality employment. While one particular technology used to last a lifetime, faster and faster changes require more and quicker essential ADAPTATION now and even more so, going forward. Not just changing "jobs" but the need to change "careers" multiple times. While a vinyl recording used to last for a generation, look how quickly we have gone through the cassette, the cd, the MP-3, the jump drive, and the download.

The same can be said about the "secret" to Adaptation: Location, Location, Location! Winners at surviving life have always moved away from danger and towards opportunity. Most times with a fair amount of risk and uncertainty but as the saying goes: "NO risk, NO Adaptation"!

Additionally, my Grandfather (without much formal education) used to say, "Eat a little bit of dirt every day to build your immunity" (Is not the basis of Homeopathic Medicine?) Although I self- identify as 'Heteropathic' ;-D). It may seem gross or tedious or even crude, but he lived until 96, not because of a 'pure' lifestyle but because of a strong (and Adaptive) immune system. You are what you eat so, in addition to having your body build against the bad, it is also important to build immunity with the 'good' stuff. Not talking fast food here but talking about nature's healing and protecting ingestibles (E.g., zinc). Instead of waiting for the face masks to be delivered via FedEx, (or to be 'saved' by some Governmental agency) why not take charge of what one can control, his or her 'insides.' It is the strong (immune vitamin "D"?) who survives, right? You do not mind if I define "strong" as a synonym for "Adaptable," do you?

Finally, there certainly are many both healthy and unhealthy relationship options for us to choose from. Quite simply. Most people are terrified of Adapting and if someone among them is not terrified, the common response is, to try and bring others down to their 'safe' level. Sticking with the "devil" we know rather than RISK the Un-known. The true "Adapters" (maybe not the pioneers) do, in fact, very much need others in their lives. But they need to surround themselves with supportive, nurturing and most of all, healthy relationships as a crucial part of their Adaptative 'team.' Bad choices in the area of relationships can only produce the 'negative' energy to hinder any necessary Adaptation.

VARIABLE AGILITY ABILITY-

This is about as good a phrase as any to summarize what I am proposing are the new essential basics of 'education' in order to be best equipped to succeed on one's OWN terms. The world has been getting 'smaller' since its existence but never more so than now. Likewise, the speed at which things must happen has never been so fast and therefore, I think the world can be divided up into either the "Agile or the Dead." By dead (obsolescent), I can mean either/and career death, ancestry death (no kids), emotional death or, even spiritual death long before any actual physical death. I realize that the kind of Agility that I am talking about will not be possible for most. Any educational talent or knowledge has always been reserved for the privileged minority. We have just gotten used to it being a middle-class activity but that has only been since Baby Booming.

The good news is that, just like the "3 R's," much of this can be self-taught to some functional degree. Naturally, a formal structure makes it easier and of a higher accomplishment plateau, but not everybody is destined for the top 'quintile.' Such a small minority of people can dunk a basketball, kick a 50-yard field goal, drive a golf ball 300 yards, throw a baseball 90 miles per hour, solve a quadratic equation or sing 3 octaves. So, why should we think EVERYONE will be able to have the human Agility necessary to become a human 'all-star'? With a shift in emphasis to the areas mentioned above, however, more of life's students might be able to do their own possible 'best.' Like for many of us playing touch football in the backyard, shooting free-throws at the YMCA, hitting from the "white tees," balancing our checkbook, playing softball as a weekend warrior, or singing "Happy Birthday" in tune, as it were, which might be the best we can achieve or even hope for?

There will always be the self-taught (school of "hard knocks"), streetwise survivors who are lucky enough to be just Agile enough. I, for one, would like to leave less of our collective survival rate to chance and formalize the process to increase the total odds through the in-place, education system. Ideally, there would be specific courses which would deal with these topics individually. I am enough of a realist to doubt that can happen in this lifetime. However, there are ways that can happen without sending the establishment Boards of Trustees around the country into cardiac arrest. Topics like "creativity," "ethics" "communication" "diversity" and "globalization" are critical elements contained within many subject disciplines. Likewise, the aspects of being Flexible, Versatile, Adjustable, and Adaptable could easily be incorporated into many of our social science type courses. By requiring these "Variable" abilities in papers, projects, team assignments and tests, students can learn to recognize the importance of these factors regardless of the topic. With the right belief, spirit, and disposition, I would think teachers of arts, sciences, education, business, and healthcare could also find ways to include these into their curricula as well. Like any other class at every level of learning, not everyone will make the Honor Roll, but each student should get as much as they can/want which is certainly more than they are getting now and at least a portion of what they will need later. This precious ability is to be able to "take ANYTHING as it comes" and deal with it accordingly. I realize that equipping students for "INTER-dependence" is not as tidy and politically palpable as slogans like: "No student left behind" but it should work better than either extreme of Societal DE-pendence (Communism?) or Learn the 'Hard Way' and create total IN-dependence (isolation?).

ON-LINE IS REALLY OUT-OF-LINE

If Management is cruising around to show off your fancy new car then, Leadership is letting a friend drive it before you buy your first tank of gas.

Despite the fact that those who, "can-NOT Teach…DO!" ;-D, Teachers are probably destined to follow the analogous plight of live-playing Musicians.

There seems to be a strong parallel between the recent on-line Education system technologies and the past technology system of Music recording. Before the phonograph, the audio tape, the cd, the MP3 and the digital download, the only way to hear Music was to go to any club, stage, amphitheater, or town square bandshell to hear the Musicians play live. It might be a quartet, a combo, an orchestra, a symphony, or a soloist but it was a real-time, three-dimensional experience between the Musicians and the audience. It was very much a two-way relationship which created deep, long-lasting, high-quality experiences and impressions. It reminds me of when I am up in front of a classroom 'performing' for a group of students immersed in the giving and taking of an open, Educational exchange.

I will not be surprised at all by the ability of <u>anyone</u> to be Educated on-line, at any distance, from sources that will be more easily accessed, less expensive and of a substantially better quality than they are now. After all, the competition from those on-line ONLY (for-profit?) institutions have steadily increased since the inception of the University of Phoenix. Additionally, more 'traditional' colleges and universities have entered the arena over the last few years with increased course options and will undoubtedly continue to do so with greater frequency and diversity. Dare I say that this type of business model is inevitable in order for traditional institutions just to survive. We seem far away from saturation point at this time, and no one seems to think there are any diminishing returns…as of yet.

In our free market economy, what will this mean? Since I do not fancy myself any sort of prognosticator, I merely suggest that we look back at the fate of the Musicians' career to offer one (scary) possibility. Once recording was invented, there became less and less opportunities for Musicians to play 'live' and fewer and fewer occasions for audiences to listen "in-person." Advantages of recorded Music to the listener are obvious: lower cost; less time investment; controlled conditions; repeat play; time-shifting, more variety, etc. An A-synchronous experience, as it were. Some would suggest a less qualitative experience, however. Over the last one hundred years, tremendous advances have been made in the area of quality by hundreds of inventors and companies. From mono to stereo, from analogue to digital, from quad to surround sound, from vinyl to tape, from live to studio to lip-sync and back to live, from speakers to ear buds, and from tweeter to sub-woofer just to name a few. Likewise, I see the same kind of advances being made in the arena of distance Education. When will "Zooming" become a verb like "Googling" has become? Much like recording went from a product to an industry, "Face Time" virtual learning is well on its way but far from the end of its innovative development.

As Marshall McLuhan said: "The Medium is the Message" and that has been certainly true in Music. Since no new Musical notes have been invented, the innovation has seemed to come from the instrumentation playing those notes. A "C" chord first played on the piano, then harpsichord, then organ, then synthesizer, then 'sampled' and yet, is still a "C" chord, unchanged in pitch. The tendency has been for Music to have become more science and less art as time progresses. The advantage is that more people are capable of playing a little 'something' with much less talent, skill, and practice than in the past. So much of the final product is 'fixed' in the editing studio, anyway. Since the average listener cannot appreciate or even hear the very subtle differences performed by the true artist, the economics of the whole situation favor the almost artificially produced work of the 'amateur' at the expense of a more authentic performance of the true 'professional.' It almost begs the question: "Why dedicate all those hours over the many years of practice for such a minimal financial return on investment?" We have certainly seen a parallel development in the field of acting where advances in computer animation create less and less of a need and appreciation for the subtlety of human emoting and in turn, fewer jobs for actors. Likewise, Sports watching has predominantly moved indoors to our High-Definition, Surround-Sound, 80-inch Flatscreen sets. How will Teachers practice the "art" of their craft in order to improve if NOT in a live performance?

I guess if one's career is digital animation or a home studio recording artist "dropping" your own record, this is great news. On the other hand, if you are a person who loves the intimacy and danger of a live lecture from a real podium then, your days may be numbered. I am fully expecting the 'Amazonization' of the Teaching world as a 'clearing house' for courses will emerge for the benefit of student selection and profit for the top tier of the academic elite. Students will search for a course from a catalog of a wide variety of tailored disciplines from every Professor/Teacher available in the world. The book authors will get top dollar and the rest of us will have to discount our services to the point of bargain shopping. This will enrich the best, not even consider the marginal, and cause the mediocre to figuratively cut each other's financial throats. Many will not have the 'stomach' for it and will leave voluntarily (or get literally "fired") and for many in future generations, a career in any kind of Teaching will not even be of much con-sideration as it would have fallen off most Guidance Counselors' 'radars.'

With an interest in some sort of editorial "rigor," let me proceed to analyze the hypothesized parallel situation between Music and Teaching using my favorite Organizational academic paradigm, Bolman and Deal's "Four Frames" assessment model.

Commencing with the Structural Frame, let us first look at some of the similarities and differences of the **Goals/Objectives** of each discipline. Both Music (as a universal language) and Education (as a benefit not a right) originally existed as non-essential 'luxuries' (for the rich and privi-leged) of life meant for the benefit of both the givers and receivers of the performance delivery. Both Music and Education can be either self-taught or formally taught although a "status" difference might exist between the two. For example, a Musician who cannot read Music (I.e., plays by 'ear'/feel) might be considered "inferior" to some "readers" of music (Music 'snobs'?) regardless of ability. Likewise, a non-certified Teacher (E.g., without Masters) who Teaches at a private school might also be considered "less than" by some of the public school establishment without regard for the 'quality' of his/her work.

Both professions have an intent to 'move' their audience with the effect of both the form and the substance of the material. Musicians can play solo but more likely, can have a greater impact as a 'team.' Teachers work almost entirely solo but if one considers the context of a "school," the team analogy seems to resonate as well. Both professions have chosen to 'organize' through "unions" in order to protect themselves from exploitation. Certainly, it is acknowledged that Teaching is now classified as one of society's "essential services" while Music is considered NON-essential (but should be) by all but the most 'enlightened.' Both share types of network communities across a 'membership' of sorts united/fortified by somewhat of a devalued and minority status. I. e. "Those who cannot do, TEACH!" Musicians "PLAY Music," as opposed to a real WORK job, like it is only a "game" of some sort.

The Political Frame is one that deals with **Conflict and Power**. There needs to be an orchestra conductor, an ensemble leader, and a Rock Band Boss (and yes, I mean Bruce Springsteen) just like there must be Department Heads, Administrators, School Principals and District Superintendents in order for things to run properly(?). Even without artistic temperaments, inflated Egos, and matter-of-principle 'fights,' when only ONE choice can be made from a palette of possibilities, there are going to be difference-of-opinion conflicts and power struggles. Music has a number of formidable Political organizations exercising considerable power its members. Everything from the 1950's "pay-for-play" ("payola") to Music Company 'forced' employee voting for Awards Shows demonstrate that Politics are alive and well in the world of Music. Likewise, every school district is run by a "Board of Trustees" who must run Political campaigns in order to get appointed/nominated/elected and in turn, control much of the working lives for Teachers.

So much of each of these 'outputs' are judged "subjectively" in nature. There is no formula for good or bad Music/Teaching and each persons' rubric for evaluation is unique. There is no manual of uniformity, no "Ten Commandments," no Agreement of right/wrong or good/bad just like in any other Political venture. Both professions tend to attract 'diva' behaviors and narcissistic demands where "personality" can carry a large weight of the totality. A caution, however, for those who are quick to concede these factors are more of an occurrence in entertainment, one might need to attend a couple of Faculty meetings. ;-D

The Human Resource Frame deals primarily with **Needs** although, in the world we live in, it is a fine line between "Wants" and actual Needs. Certainly, physicality and maybe spirituality, but Music and Teaching each definitely produce "outcomes" which contain both an intellectual component and an emotional component. These vary greatly in proportion depending on style/subject of the best practitioners. For example, Classical Musicians might employ a ratio of 90% 'head' and 10% 'heart' (like 'Hard' Sciences?) while for the "Blues", it might be the exact opposite of 90% 'heart' and 10% 'head' (like Fine Arts?). Jazz players might be 50%/50%? (like Business/Health Care?). Country Music is like (down) Home Economics; Hard Rock is like "Shop;" and Pop is like Phys Ed. O.P.K. (only partially kidding) and L.T.M. (Laughing to Myself).

Despite the levity, much of Music (through hard work by Musicians) is designed and meant for enjoyment (passive listening, sensory reflecting and relaxing). On the other hand, Education when done correctly, requires hard work on behalf of BOTH the Educators AND of the 'students' (reading, writing, testing) to be an "active" listener and using critical thinking which, are hardly relaxing. In either case, most Musicians and Teachers often describe their choice of career as some sort of "calling." I remember reading a bumper sticker once which read: "Have You Ever Heard of a Teacher Quitting to Do Something MORE Important?" It is also common to hear about Musicians who have given up many of life's' customs and conventions

(I. e. starving for their art) to keep their 'dream' alive. There are certainly more financial benefits for the extremely successful (star) Musician vis-à-vis the successful Teacher, but the top Educators can certainly do very well financially also. E.g., Research One University "grants," patent "royalties," textbook "income."

The Symbolic Frame is the "Big Daddy" of the Four Frames. It can have the most importance and the most influence because it creates all of The **Meaning** for its 'affected.' The Culture in which all of us live may be hard to define but we know what it is when we experience it. There have been times when both Music and Teaching have been elevated to high priorities in various Cultures and times when each was downgraded in importance. It might be hard to correlate when its criticality has been linked to its availability or even excellence (I.e., a "Golden Age"). Much like Advertising being cut during a recession or exercise being cut when one is tired, there may be counterintuitive planning and unintended consequences in both the area of Teaching and Music. For example, despite the causation of better math scores among students playing musical instruments in school, funding for the "Arts" has still been cut. Or Technology investments forgone in lieu of Athletic expenditures.

I have taken some 'liberties' with the 4, separate Frames and have created why I call the "Fifth Frame" to help describe some of the dynamics which can happen BETWEEN the individual frames. There may be cases when two or more Frames mix to form something neither "fish nor fowl." Other times, a unique but clearly identifiable combination emerges the way that a perfect "pink" emerges from mixing Red and White. Since the best of all possible situations is a harmonious 'balance' among all the Frames, being able to identify any noteworthy Dominance and/or Weakness can be helpful to any analysis and recommendations.

A similarity between Teaching and Music which I find powerful is how each generation needs its own 'representatives' to speak the same classic 'truths.' A young generation wants to hear about (the same) "love" from contemporaries of their own choosing and students want to learn the same basic life "lessons" (E.g., biology) from Teachers with whom they can relate (like children listening and believing non-related adults (E.g., aunts) rather than their own moms/dads) . For all but a very few Musicians, they seem to lose 'credibility' with aging at a much faster rate than Teachers. Professors who, after cease being "cool" at least have a chance to return as old and wise. Musicians seem to get devalued as they age. **Human Resource mixing equally with Symbolic.**

Another factor which seems to cross Frame boundaries is the many 'sub-groups' within each discipline and the inter-disciplinary competition existing amongst them. For example, within the University there exist certain friendly 'rivalries' between the Arts & Science College and the Professional Schools (Business, Education, Health Science). Arts/Sciences oftentimes position themselves as the older, more pure, and strictly academic group versus colleagues and their students "studying" for the purpose of job acquisition. Just as Classical players might feel 'superior' to (it's good enough for) Rock & Roll players. Since there is a little "Truth in every Tease," status like tenure, promotion and awards can hinge on some of these distinctions. **Political potentially dominating the Structural.**

Another observation is about the many different LEVELS within each profession. Do Teachers have the same prestige level whether Teaching grade school, high school, technical/junior college or at the University? This may be subject to much interpretation and some debate. I think it very much depends on each particular individual. I, for one, get rather good student evaluations from 18-22 year-old students but I think I would be terrified (and do poorly) with pre-teenage students. So, does higher necessarily mean better? In my case, at least, a healthy "Yes!" A similar discussion can be had regarding the differences between Recording Studio Musicians versus Live-Playing Musicians and/or small-group (band) Musicians versus large-group (orchestra) Musicians. **Human Resource informing Structural with a 'hint' of Symbolic.**

Furthermore, there can be many status levels within and among both professions. For example "Research 1" Institutions often emphasize Journal Publishing over actual Teaching and usually can pay more money than "teaching" schools. Professors can 'buy' their way out of Teaching assignments with "grants" (for Doctoral Candidates to substitute) much the same way that the 'best' studio Musicians can play on the "recording" while leaving the grueling road tour for 'lesser' Musicians to "copy" their 'parts' every night on stage. Just as Musicians have different potential contributions to be made to the "Music" (performing/writing/producing it), Teachers have the different contributions of Instructing; Service and Research/Administration to make. **Political and Symbolic affecting Structural and Human Resource**.

Also, within the ranks of each profession we find interesting internal dynamics. Quite often, we might see personality similarities associated with particular positions and both Official and Unofficial "Leadership" within organizations. For example, a "lead" guitarist can be different in both ability and personality than a "rhythm" guitarist. Usually more extroverted and the best have been described as "having a separate 'brain' in each finger." Conversely, I remember the old joke: "what do you call a person who hangs around with MUSICIANS all of the time?"-A DRUMMER! Despite the disparaging remarks, anyone who has ever tried to keep a different rhythmic pattern with each of their four appendages, would certainly beg to differ. Many times, a more 'cerebral' type person will be drawn to the keyboards and serve in the "Musical Director/Arranger"-type position. We can see similar types of relationships within the Academy. "Senior" Faculty can exert both Official and Unofficial Leadership amongst his/her colleagues. Either by taking positions in the Administration (E.g., Provost) or through Dean/Committee-Chair service to influence various processes. At the other end of the spectrum, tenure-seeking "junior" Faculty may not get the 'out-front' visibility of any "solos" but have to do the 'heavy lifting' ("publish or perish") while remaining out of the 'spotlight.' At least for the present time, the "Hard" skills of Math and Science (numbers) seem to more 'status'/prestige than the so called "Soft" skills of Words and Feelings. Maybe the way that Symphony members compare to Lounge bands? **Structural exerting Political over Symbolic and Human Resource.**

Additionally, both Teachers and Musicians can have "larger-than-life" meaning to both fans and students alike. Many of us mark events/periods in our lives with a Musical reference (E.g., importance in movies). Musicians can compensate for any emotional/spiritual limitations that WE might have in our ability to express ourselves properly/fully. Likewise, many Teachers can a significant influence (career choice, geographic location, etc.) life choices like very few other people, sometimes even more than family, friends, or celebrities. To a NON aficionado, all of a Musician's work can sound the 'same.' To a true devotee, even the most subtle variations can take on entirely different meanings. Same work, entirely distinct interpretations. Also true with Teachers, the exact lecture, at the same time, can be both inspiring and boring depending on the style of the teacher and the receptivity of the pupil. **Symbolic having significant Influence upon Human Resource.**

Back to our original premise, are Teachers destined to follow the same evolutionary decline as Musicians in their journey from a live, in-person profession to one being replaced by technology? Just as there is really "Nothing New Under the Musical Sun" as far as 'content' (notes/chords) is concerned then, all of the innovation has to come from new 'forms' (instrumentation). Likewise, the vast majority of Teaching utilizes existing material and just re-arranges, re-organizes, and re-prioritizes alternative combinations of the same language. Research is a different category altogether (although much of it is derivative to some extent and can be mostly 'recycled') and not in the same 'danger' as the actual 'live' Teaching (unless Artificial Intelligence really comes a long way). I would certainly be remiss not to acknowledge this swapping of jobs-for-technology has been rampant since intersection traffic police have been replaced by "stoplights" (are they not really "stop, caution & go" lights?). So many 'agent'-type jobs have been replaced by technology and so many 'production'-type jobs have been replaced by automation. With Artificial Intelligence (A. I.) 3-D robots hovering nearby, I am just sounding the 'alarm' about the Teaching profession. Much like Music, it has an extremely special place in my life. I know it can even get worse as I have heard that the single biggest financial opportunity for A.I. is in the area of female sexual surrogates, I.e., 'blow-up dolls' come to "life."

Let us look at the "synthesizers" for example. Since its 'perfection,' one keyboard and its player can **replace** entire brass horn sections, string sections, woodwinds, and any other keyboard (organ, piano, harpsichord, etc.) as well as the Musicians who play them. Certainly, this presents no problem for recording whatsoever as recording is now both multi-track and digital. It may be a little less convenient in a "live" setting but possible, nonetheless. The same can be said for so-called "drum machines." Not only can they replace any and all percussion instrumentation and players but like all automation robots, some claim they actually play "better" by being more "precise" than Humans. The counter argument is that machines lack the "feel" of a drummer but in many other areas of work life, 'employers' feel the trade-off is worth the cost savings (E.g., no sick time; vacation days; coffee breaks; bad moods; governmental imposed taxes; etc.).

I see the exact same things happening in the field of Education. With the changes in both video and audio, (better, smaller, portable, cheaper), the opportunities to "record" lectures are just too tempting. Just as one would always prefer to hear a favorite song by its originator sometimes we will 'settle' for the case of a "cover," by the **best** player available (or one's personal choice). Why would anyone want to listen to an inferior performance recording if possible? Likewise, if the author of the textbook is willing to record his/her lecture about a given topic, why would anyone want to listen to anyone's "second-hand" interpretation lecture, especially for the same cost? If one cannot afford to see the author of the song or of the book, one might be willing to 'compromise' on a 'surrogate' for less money. See the "writing on the wall here?" Good, old 'regular' Teachers will have to discount their services until the point when one might have to PAY students to listen to THEIR lectures. J.ust K.idding…for now!

Like books-on-tape beforehand, it is not only the technology of mobile audio and video "A-synchronous" recording at work here on places like BlackBoard. As the 'Zooming'/"Facetime"/"Teams" of the world gets better, the give-and-take, question-and-answer "Synchronous" component of on-line and distant learning will enable even more realistic participation for those who want it. Although, I am fully suspecting that the textbook authors will have their "Graduate" students actually host the "Q & A" sessions as well as still do the grading. (sarcasm, resentment, and bitterness intended). I guess this will be the Educational equivalent of Musicians 'lip-synching' to pre-recorded (Tupac Shakar hologram performance?) Music while on a television show? But not only is there a recording/play-back component to all of this but an "editing"/special effects technology aspect which will be able to create almost 'Hollywood' production value for those able to afford it. The poorer Teachers and/or schools, however, will draw as stark of a comparison as a "black & white" broadcast is to a 'color' rendition.

The argument here is all about consumer options. Even though a more critically acclaimed version of a song may exist in recorded form, there are many people who might prefer hearing a song played live, in-person by non-award winning Musicians (actual songwriter's 'night') just for the 'qualitative' experience of it. As that choice has become much more difficult to obtain and available much less often, Musicians have fewer opportunities to do what they love or practice getting better. As with anything, the truly gifted and very wealthy will not suffer and, on the contrary, will do better than ever before. Likewise the destitute and un-talented will do no WORSE (untenable) than ever before. My concern is for the 'average' player who was satisfied with a modest income from relative mediocrity. They are gone or will very soon be gone!

The same can be said for Teachers. There are many, many Teachers and Professors who do a just a fine job in a "live' performance. Many students might enjoy a live lecture from an 'average' instructor more than a video from the world's foremost authority. Will that student's choice be whittled down to "all or nothing" much the same manner in which many Musicians have suffered their fate? When dealing with Human Nature, no one has enough resources (time, money, energy) to satisfy all of their wants. Give people the choice between cake and veggies and they will choose cake. Given the choice between hard work/most benefit and easy work/less benefit most will choose "phoning it in." I fear that the average educators will get swept away somewhere between the best and the worst, just like what has happened to Musicians.

Of course, this will not happen in any type of "rapture" but rather slowly and painfully subject-by-subject, Teacher-by-Teacher, school-by-school. Much like "Popular" Music changes from generation to generation, "majors" and courses change to suit the 'times.' Classical Music has lost much of its audience in the same manner in which the "Classic" subjects of Greek and Latin have lost most of its students. Current majors seemed to be directed towards those areas which can result in gainful employment upon graduation (I.e., economic realities of paying off student loans). Just as there is not much demand for "Ragtime" or "Zither" Music these days, I wonder how much practical demand there will be for NON-pragmatic courses (E. g. Philosophy) when the "unaffordable economic realities" of "brick-and-mortar" classrooms hit with full force?

WILL IT COME DOWN TO WOMEN VERSUS MEN?

*If Management is strongly voicing your opinion/views then,
Leadership is listening openly to understand all the
opinions/views of everybody.*

The World has always known its adversarial conflicts throughout history, and it usually produces distinct victors, at least for a short, celebratory period of time. We have seen more than our share of fatal conflicts based on differences of religion, culture, ethnicity, resources, power, class/caste, economics, race, age, education, employment, perceptions, perspectives, beliefs, ideologies, philosophies, governments, values, morals, ethics, laws, geographical territories and maybe even psychographics. However, have we ever finally come to the point when we are willing to pit Men against Women in a winner-take-all gender war? It seems to me that we might be heading down that path.

Unlike many of the differences resulting from the above (and I hope exhaustive) list, Women and Men are unlike each other at the most basic level. Whether you believe in God Creation, Intelligent Design, Darwinian evolution or just total randomness, each person is born either male or female. There may be degrees along a continuum, but nature makes an either/or choice. One may identify differently, have various sexual orientations, or even surgically/chemically alter one's gender but that does not change the initial reality of birth. Some people might not give too much importance to that original fact these days but that does not change the most basic way in which people are differentiated. Not prioritized mind you, just distinctly classified (I.e., vagina or penis…is it just COINCIDENCE that, they fit together in order to produce offspring?). It is probably not healthy for any side to become hypersensitive to this issue; less any differences become distorted UN-reasonability.

Whether you categorize by genitalia, chromosomes, or any other physical characteristic, all I am suggesting is that mere biology makes males and females unable ever to be <u>exactly</u> the same. (x & y chromosomes?). I understand that there may be more potential for some overlap in our spiritual, emotional, intellectual, and psychological natures but not in our fundamental physical nature. To state even more primordially, there may even be some overlap in physical characteristics of dermatological, muscular, skeletal, hormonal and many organ components. ONLY Women however can carry and deliver offspring from an egg in a uterus and Men cannot. Likewise, ONLY Men can produce sperm from their testes and Women cannot. Even though there are now formula substitutes for infant feeding, I am also quite sure that only Female nipples/breasts can suckle infants. There may be less emphasis on those capabilities these days vis-à-vis other human dimensions (E.g., work success) nevertheless, that difference still remains. As such, we cannot completely ignore this underlying difference, although this can never give license to disparage, devalue, or harass either gender, obviously.

Without making any judgments, we cannot completely ignore our connection to nature as human animals. Yes, I know that it is somewhat primal, and we all have higher natures and should operate mostly from a position as enlightened beings. The answer is **not** using spirit, emotion, and intellect at the <u>exclusion</u> of the physical but in conjunction and concert with those more sublime aspects. It is true that we rule the animal world due to our superior brain, but I do not think that gives us permission to ignore the dimensions of our other human traits. For example, our emotional aspect helps us to differentiate the act of making love versus just having sex. Additionally, our spiritual aspect helps us to make a monogamous commitment to our spouse despite any temptations to the widespread scattering of our seed. Finally, our physical aspect of the testosterone/estrogen blend might determine whether we prefer to hunt or nest and whether we come from

Venus or Mars. Regardless if our definition of beauty is Ruben-esque or heroin-chic, Men have always tried to chase (one's perception of) attractive Women for sexual satisfaction and whether our definition of strong is gladiator/square-chin or sensitive/funny/smart, Women have always tried to lure healthy Men for procreation/protection. When did the battle of the sexes become so toxic?

I can certainly empathize with all those who have pushed for women's equality from suffrage through liberation, but I fear (for the women) that collectively, they may now be over-shooting the mark. By that, I simply mean that there is a natural tendency for all people who feel oppressed to want to make up for time lost and/or overcompensate for any perceived deserved inequities. Please remember that the farthest tail of the bell curve can be as BAD as the nearest tail of the bell curve as far as healthy balance is concerned. First of all, the terms equality and sameness are not synonymous. In other words, we ALL want a fair, equitable and just distribution of life's rights/benefits but I think expecting People to need the <u>exact</u>, same things is a mistaken oversimplification. If you consider the world's Oldest Profession, is it mere randomness that, the overwhelming majority of suppliers are Women and the overwhelming majority of demanders are Men? Our sexual needs/wants may not be the <u>only</u> ones but they seem to be THE ones for whom both Men and Women have been willing to risk everything from fortune, career, family and even throne. Applying equitability takes a lot more wisdom and effort than creating equality. The purveyors of gender equality seem to be NO more concerned with their consumers' welfare than advertisers are in the verity of their selling messages. You decide for yourselves where you rank the intended outcomes of these purveyors. I personally place them right in the middle of the pantheon of all other salespeople…turning WANTS into NEEDS.

My point of view may be influenced by the fact that, I have always felt Women are in NO way inferior to Men and in many respects are probably in fact, **superior**. I have always believed that the best talent, most ability, and biggest contribution to humankind is the ability to perpetuate (I.e., carry in utero) the human race. Without the ability to give birth to babies, the world would cease to exist in about a hundred years. I know that women need a man's sperm to fertilize (artificially?) their egg, but I think some female animals in nature have figured out how get pregnant without males and I wonder if that could also happen with humans? The best nature can do with males is to parent born offspring like the penguins or carry a female's eggs like seahorses. So no, I do not think that it is a Man's World (apologies to James Brown). After a lifetime of working in a variety of corporate profit environments and academic non-profit environments, I can even state that, I have much more respect for the home keeping duties of the traditional homemaker than many of the things that I have done to earn a living. After all, should we not value taking care of family much more highly than taking care of customers/clients/patients? I take an ultimate pride and satisfaction in any and all family contributions that I am able to make on behalf of my wife and children. I think many women have been "brainwashed" to think LESS of domestic responsibilities and to think MORE of potential global, professional career opportunities. Maybe it is time for people of all genders to be 'heart-washed' or even more important-ly, 'soul-washed.' For example, do we ever think to 'factor' the need of the male human species to "care for and protect" the female human species? Will the extinction of that need/desire cause unintended consequences that humankind will live to regret despite all of women's self-sufficiency?

Anyone who has ever seen a Mother's Love at work knows that a Father can move mountains for their children and yet **never, ever** hold as special of a place in their life as Mom. Rather, it seems more likely to me that, on some level Men used their aggression in things like Business, War, Sports, and maybe even domestic abuse (consciously or subconsciously) in order to <u>compensate</u> for the inability to perform the greatest of all Human tricks – birth (which creates that unique, one-of-a-kind love between Mom and child). I am sure that there are as many Men who want to be Fathers as there are Women who want to be Mothers. To any Man who is looking to reproduce, it certainly seems that Women have absolutely ALL of the **POWER** in the process. To put it in the terms of supply and demand, mar-ket conditions or scare resources, a high-quality donor can sell her single, egg for upwards of $50,000 (plus expenses) while the best a man can do is sell a couple Billion sperm for around $100 (plus visual stimulus). Please do not think that I am trying to objectify either Men or Women by this example but just place a perspective on relative value.

I certainly do NOT subscribe to/accept many of the gender differences explained in any of the original religious writings. I think this is more because a Woman had to invest **nine** long, hard, and dangerous **months** while pregnant and a Man had a lot of time after investing only about **nine minutes** (giving us the benefit here) in the act of procreation. Thus, leaving a Man with a lot of time/energy to write an explanation of things from HIS perspective. Everyone writes everything from an egocentric, self-serving purpose and a Man was just in a better position to author HIS-story. The hard part is for people to know what should and should not be changed as life in this world evolves. I find it hard <u>NOT</u> to blame the purveyors of ideas, which benefit (financially) themselves at the expense of the honest, trusting, and decent folks whose only fault is being willing to follow. Human Nature comprises those folks who exploit it and those folks (minority) who advocate for those with less capacity for comprehension. I know certain people can psychologically manipulate wants into needs for those who are not able to contain/restrain themselves (I.e., naive?). It is normal Human Nature to want things we cannot have and to think that having those things will make us happier. It is also normal Human Nature to think that the grass is always greener on the other side. I believe that is really, what is at work here, Many Women think that Men have it **better** than they do because they have been sold a "bill-of-bads." I for one, think they are lusting after fool's gold.

The biggest threat to love, intimacy, companionship, and procreation as I see it is a **lack** of need for each other's differences between Men and Women. If we become too much alike, I think we will **repel** each other and NOT **attract** each other, just like magnets. Little-by-little, slowly-but-surely, we are creating situations of total INDEPENDENCE, whereby neither gender needs the other…at all! I am <u>not</u> suggesting that we return to the bad arrangement of Women's complete DEPENDENCE upon Men, but

I am suggesting that as a Human Race, we should strive for conditions of INTERDEPENDENCE and not either extreme. I read that one of the biggest economic opportunities in the area of Artificial Intelligence (A.I.) is in that of sexual surrogates for men. The idea being that, if robots can replace human women for sexual needs, there may be less of an interest in Men to have a need with Women for any kind of relationship at all! To put it in chauvinistic and crude terms, (which some, not me, might think/feel/believe): "why put up with all of the nagging, if I no longer need to get laid?"

Conversely, if Women are able to have any job that any man can have, then they may see no need to respect, trust or even want what ANY Man can provide for a relationship. Since Men cannot PRODUCE children, many have suggested that Men really need to PRODUCE at work, job, career, profession, etc. Without a Man's ability to do that, I am not sure if He can see much purpose in living. If Women can both PRODUCE children as well as any work they want to PRODUCE, I am not sure what purpose/benefit they would see in a relationship with a Man. Maybe a steep rise in same-gender relationships? Okay Ladies, I concede, YOU win! YOU can do it **all** and WE cannot. So what might happen? Well, maybe the best human Female specimens will be totally fulfilled with all of the top, Leadership positions in society, make all the money, experience increases in 'affairs,' ulcers and heart disease and may even evolve/(devolve) to 'shop' at the sperm bank if not becoming infertile. Those genetics might be less likely to pass down and contribute to survival of the fittest. The best human Male specimens will waste all of their high-quality sperm on sex androids, waste all of their money on drinking, golfing, and gambling with their buddies and never own more than a 'man cave' in one of the new, man-cave sub-divisions. Their good traits might also die out along the evolutionary highway. What might be left for posterity then? The worst and the dimmest. It is quite possible that the only people reproducing are the Men who cannot afford robots and the Women who cannot get great jobs. De-evolution at its finest. Sounds extreme unless you consider it happening slowly over hundreds of years.

Maybe another word or two about a couple of current controversial hot topics. First on the subject of abortion. I understand that a women's body is her own she should be able to make any choice about/with that body that is a result of HER action alone. The distinction with pregnancy, however, is that she cannot reach the condition of pregnancy on HER OWN without a sperm (from either man or 'bank'). At least at this point, she cannot yet get/become pregnant by herself and therefore needs to decide/act in concert with at least the Father and probably societal laws, whatever they might be. For my own particular conscience, life begins at conception but for my intellect, I can accept it would have to begin either when egg is fertilized OR when a first breath is taken. Any other period during those 10 months seems very arbitrary and subject to many political and/or religious agendas. Both parties must be responsible for unwanted children through birth control/prevention as well as all born babies. Is it really HER body to do what she wants with if she cannot produce a fetus alone? She is the essential vessel, but can she control MORE than just her body without any input from the sperm donor? I guess the REAL issue is not just between a person and a doctor but ultimately between a person and their maker (God). If one believes in any "Creator" at all, the LEAST of one's problems is from the any government of this world and any legislation pales in comparison to "Judgment Day."

On the subject of sports, I think this is a classic "apples and oranges" comparison. In most competitive endeavors, Women and Men can be evaluated against common criteria. For example, if one is selling cars, either gender can make the exact same amount of money (provided there is no commission discrimination). If a Man and a Woman are both scientists seeking a cure for cancer, I am sure either gender would reap the acclaim or financial rewards for success most equally. Even in soldiering, bullets and bombs can kill indiscriminately. I know, I know there are the issues of opportunities and access, but those issues are quickly going away. All you have to do is look at the visibility of Women in the media/politics to see that changing on a daily basis. In sports, however, UNTIL the best individual Woman or Women's team BEATS (unlikely due only to inherent 'physicality' differences, NOT Human Worth differences) the best individual Man or Men's team head-to-head, there can be no ultimate victory in terms of financial and/or accomplishment equality. In fact, while parity might seem at hand for Wimbledon Men's and Women's tennis champions with equal purses, since Men Champions have to win the best of **five** sets and Women only have to win best of **three** sets, the Women actually earn 50% **MORE** per won set! The "fairer sex" certainly out negotiated the white tennis shorts off the Men on that one.

The whole Trans-Gender issue will be left for the someone much smarter than me to figure out.

A lot is made these days of the tremendous need for and lack of Leadership around the world, most pertinently in the United States of America. As someone who teaches Leadership at the university level, I thought I might weigh in on that subject as well. Most experts would agree that a significant difference exists between the requirements for the discipline of Management as compared to those of Leadership. Many have even suggested that traditional female traits (nurturing, sensitivity, tolerance, openness, etc.) are much better suited for the demands of Leaders than those natural tendencies of the masculine gender. Likewise, those traditional male traits of aggression, shorter-term measurements, single-minded focus, bottom-line mentality, etc. are better served within the scope of the Management profession. So, what then is the problem? As I see it, the fly-in-the-ointment, chink-in-the-armor, monkey-wrench-in-the-gears is POLITICS. Most Leaders achieve their position through a process which relies heavily on political components/factors. Power (the fuel of the political engine) is almost antithetical to Leadership and is most always counterproductive for true Leaders. So here in a 'nutshell' is the DIS-connect; Politics is a game best played by Manager types and Men are generally better suited for both Management AND Politics. We need to appoint Women to positions of Leadership by ACCLAIMATION and not de-base Leaders (People) by subjecting them to the Political machinations. My guess is that those people best suited for Leadership roles are not interested in doing what is necessary (antithetical to inherent Leadership values) to wage and win a Political Campaign.

If the current global era is marked by polarization whereby extreme positions are the only ones that an overwhelming majority of people are willing/able to take then, most people will ultimately head for diametrically opposed corners with their myopic blinders firmly in place. I know that it is much easier to see the world in absolute blacks & whites but whatever wisdom we have has been has shown us that, only tenable places to exist are in shades of gray. Since I believe most Human Nature is inherently lazy, we cling to our bias,' our stereotypes,' our bigotry, and our bounded rationality in order to satisfice with our generalizations and justifications. It is easier/less time-consuming to vote the party line than to learn each individual position on every issue for all of the candidates. Just imagine if Caucasians (European-Americans?) and African Americans had NEVER been called White and Black but rather Beige and Brown? We might just see ourselves as slight gradations of the same color family and not associate any group with the opposites of lightness (better?) and darkness (worse?).

I am sure that Men find it easier to trash Women in the locker room rather to work to understand them. Likewise, Women would rather exasperate themselves trying to 'change' Men than exert the effort to accept them as they are. Why not comprehend the 95% genetic similarity between the sexes and not obsess over that lousy 5% difference? Is patience not more important than six-pack abdominal muscles? Is tolerance not more important than silicone implants? The middle ground (Equal but Different) is the ONLY hallowed ground for the Genders! We all need to get a damn grip and to move further away from the baseness of our Human Nature and closer to the spirit of our Divine Nature.

LAWS ARE SO 20TH CENTURY

*If Management is seeing an overweight person and thinking,
"How Lazy?" then, Leadership is helping one discover more self-esteem.*

The United States of America prides itself on being a land of laws and <u>not</u> a land of autocratic decision makers. At the time of the Constitution's writing and probably through the end of the 1900's, I concede that rule-by-laws was innovative, worldwide news and a vast improvement upon the alternatives of monarchs, dictators, and military conquerors.

I do believe that the Legislative process has served us well until recently at the Federal, State and Local levels. I also believe that laws are a method inferior to ethical and moral governing in today's world much the same way in that analog is now inferior to digital at a time when depth, breadth, diversity, and speed rule the day.

As I see it, human evolution began merely a struggle for **PHYSICAL** survival. As such, it was dog-eat-dog and survival of the fittest in earth's jungle. Therefore, strength and speed were of paramount importance. You know, I do not have to out-run the saber-toothed tiger, just out-run or out-jump my fellow cave man. If I can also out-wrestle him, I get to mate with a female and procreate MY genetics. Bullies and bullying most likely ruled the law of that jungle.

Laws seem to emerge from the next level of evolution, the **INTELLEC-TUAL** aspect of Homo sapiens. Our superior brainpower enabled humans to dominate the animal kingdom using rational thinking to trump any of our disadvantages of physical inferiority to other animals (E.g., inventing tools and weapons). The problem, as I see it, is that once we became heads of the food chain, we turned our logical abilities against each other in a competition of shrewdness and cunning (not necessarily sincerity) in order to gain advantages of resources.

Lawyers have high intellect and lawyers make and use laws to theirs and their clients' advantage. Any legislation is created to benefit those who have the power to determine what they think is right and wrong. Since perception is reality and subjective, the definition of right and wrong is never black & white. The smartest people get to interpret all the shades of gray and/or to create a full-color world from their own perspective. Furthermore, they are able to justify it better than those who have less intellectual horsepower. Please consider the concept of "loopholes." Who can best use them? How are they used? How often are they used? Whom do they most often and best benefit?

It seems to me that, this is exactly where the world was at the time of the man, Jesus Christ. As the saying goes, there are lies, damn lies and research, which simply means that intellect alone does not guarantee any semblance of <u>truth</u>, just one's ability to sell one's own ideas. Whether we are talking about mythology, science, laws or even fake news, the intellectual approach just separates the smart from the dumb in the same way that, in physicality, the fast distance themselves from the slow or the strong impose their will upon the weak. When we think of the modern day, larger-than-life heroes, it seems that we are **NOT** most in awe of their one-dimensional intellectual capacity (most of whom eventually get proven wrong as knowledge evolves—the Earth is neither flat nor does the Sun revolve around it). Rather our admiration of their prowess transcends human brainpower bordering on the realm of the divine. Besides Jesus, people like Gandhi, Saint Mother Teresa, the Dali Lama, Martin Luther King, etc. have NOT relied on mere intellectualism to make their mark on people. They embody a much more holistic presence than just their mind.

Current times seem hauntingly reminiscent of that time when the laws took precedent over the hearts of the people of the world. Somehow, despite a noble attempt from the Hippie movement, we are still stuck in the intellectual aspect of Human development. People cannot or will not rise to the higher facet of **EMOTIONAL** enlightenment. Christ preached that the best emotion (life approach) of all was Agape Love, and he was crucified for it. The Beatles sang that, <u>All You Need is Love</u> and John Lennon was assassinated for it. It certainly is much <u>harder</u> to out-Love than to out-talk but that only means that Love is the activity more worthy than thought. It is almost unnatural to turn the other cheek when attacked but I am afraid that will be what is required to move onward and upward as human beings. I am suggesting that in lieu of drowning in data, imbibing information, and hiding behind fine print, what is needed is the Ethical treatment within each one of our organizations no matter how large or how small. This is precisely why Emotional Intelligence (E.Q.) seems to have taken the priority away from Intellectual Intelligence (I.Q.) as the main 'trait' within the world of Organizational Leadership. Ethics requires smarts that are distilled through the heart. It is as basic as the Golden Rule. Alternatively, as a mentor of mine once taught, would you be proud to support any decision in front of your Mother or while appearing on worldwide television? That used to be a decisive test of Ethics although seeing some of the lies I see perpetuated on ALL media, I am not so sure if that would be a stringent enough test anymore.

I would be thrilled if the world operated with the Ethical nature of Human Emotional interaction, but I feel compelled at least to mention the highest form of Human interaction/behavior and that would be the **SPIRITUAL** component of our collective being. This aspect is based on individual <u>Morality (I.e., concern for one's own soul)</u>. It is one's own determination of what one thinks is right or wrong and good or bad. This is so hard to influence, as it is determined at an early age by one's parental upbringing, religious indoctrination, educational influence, and social norms. It is woven into the fiber of our being and is foundational and fundamental to who we are as individuals. I think that it is particularly difficult when the world seems more determined than ever to reward the material, the superficial, the notorious, the powerful, the image conscious, the prestige segregated and the collective Branding of people/organizations over the integrity and dignity of the person and/or groups. Otherwise, why would we ever tolerate any form of bullying of another as some sort of badge of honor? Additionally, how would anyone justify generalized killing in the name of ANY religion? We have done more than missed "true North," we have lost THE compass.

If I just argued that the concept of right and wrong is subjective, how can individuals ever agree on a common set of beliefs/actions that make the world a better place when there are so many distinct cultural/semiotic influences at work? If we look to the world's religions, we might conclude that, all of them say the same basic thing on about 90% of all of the major tenets – the 'Whats'. Things like love, afterlife, family, ceremonies, celebrations, prayer, forgiveness, faith, belief, etc. Where they disagree is on the minor/finer points of the 'Hows' (E.g., denominations). In other words, all major religions spend all of their time, money, and energy on the 10% **how** (the 'means') the very same ending 90% objective is accomplished (the 'ends'). If ever there was a cart put before a horse, this seems like the textbook definition. Especially when you consider that, most religions are willing even to kill in the name of proving their point or at least to stop someone else from proving theirs.

Is not the very same condition true for all governments? Every country on earth wants prosperity, peace, culture, full employment, food, safety, healthcare, education, happiness, etc. for its entire people. That is 90% of the 'Whats', which are pretty universal. We go to war over 10% of the 'How's' or, at least the 'How Much's' (I.e., democracy, monarchy, republic, capitalism, socialism, communism). What will it take for our Leaders (or any individual) to see the forest for the trees on this? The big picture is the only one that matters from a **SPIRITUAL**/<u>Moral</u> standpoint. Nevertheless, we continue to ignore the best advice from our best religious/spiritual advisors and take the path of the short term, the 10%, the shallow, the low-hanging fruit, the easy, the immediate, the crude, the quick & dirty, etc. This undoubtedly comes at the expense of heaven on earth (however, one defines it) let alone one's after-life heaven (however, one defines it).

At the root of all religious organizations, political organizations and business organizations are people. As people, all of us succumb to our own Human Nature while falling short of the aspiration to our Divine Nature.

The little devil on one shoulder and the little angel on the other shoulder. I think it is safe to say that individuals of power, influence, money, and opportunities cannot help but listen to the little devil of temptation. After all, they have so much tangibility to gain in THIS world and only 'promises' from the NEXT life. The rest of us (Common Man) probably listen to that little angel of righteousness more often than not. Not because we are any better than others are mind you but because we have so little concrete to gain in this world and so much potentially to lose in eternity. For the meek have 'nots,' two birds in the bush are our <u>only</u> option since we do not have access to that bird in the hand like the 'haves' do. I guess the "meek" can only hope to "inherit the heaven"?

Gun control seems like a perfect example of this dilemma. When the framers of the Constitution created the Second Amendment, I doubt that anyone in the world could even imagine an automatic weapon like an AR-15. Therefore, the LAW created, as the "right to bear arms"(I.e., muscats), was appropriate and even necessary for the militia at those times in our country's history. To defend that law in the face of the ethical and moral outcomes experienced in the 21st century seems myopic and self-serving. The fact that the people who work for us taxpayers cannot or will not produce a solution other than two diametrically opposed extreme (legal) positions suggests to me that they are not competent enough at their jobs at best and "bought-and-paid-for" at the worst. By doing nothing, we are in fact saying that we are willing to lose all the lives during mass shootings as a cost of absolute freedom and have no notion of the 'spiritual' worth of those loss of lives. Maybe the Canadian model needs to be studied?

Like someone once said (paraphrasing): Anyone most capable of solving this country's problems and capitalizing on all of its opportunities would NEVER get elected because he or she would never be able to stoop to the activities necessary to conduct a winning political campaign. It is like winning an election and Leading this nation are two, diametrically opposed Human quality situations. I.e., The Spiritual Leader we desperately need would have too much more integrity, morality, and ethics than to play and win in the political arena.

THE UNITED AMERICAS OF STATE

If Management is thinking that your favorite artist/entertainer/athlete is the BEST of all time then, Leadership is knowing that every generation needs "heroes" to stimulate, express and inspire.

The current World Order vision is so obsolete that it seems 'criminal' that our current leaders are totally out-of-touch with how to organize for future survival let alone success.

The endemic structural flaw is quite simple (and obvious to me) and that is, alliances have previously been set up to position East and West (based on some ideologies/philosophies/religious beliefs as opposed to the dominant one of Geography) and now it would seem better served if the strongest alliances were set up to combine North and South.

It seems to me that the best alliances possible would be that would contain everything, and everyone included within the current continents of North America and South America from the North Pole to the South Pole.

Why am I suggesting that? Glad you asked!

- Being surrounded by two, expansive oceans provide a great defense for self-protection (and therefore, a powerful sense of security) as opposed to a fearmongering (bordering on paranoia) caused by such imagined threats such as Communism, Fascism, Jihadism, and other manufactured threats of mass destruction. Vietnam? Korea? Afghanistan? Iran? Ukraine? Palestine/West Bank, Etc.?

  - Geography (NOT Isolationism, mind you) would firmly place terrain, time, and distance as effective weapons of defense for our side against any REAL threats. I think it also precludes the need to

"

obviate any 'offensive' plans under the cloak of a phony 'defensive' rationale.

- The Americas can provide almost all of the resources (both natural and man-made) necessary for the needs/wants for all the people of the entire region concerned.

  o Thereby creating a tremendous sense of Self-Sufficiency and dare I say, true Independence.

  o Trade then becomes more of a win-win proposition and not as trade-deficit producing.

- A cooperative effort could **substitute** work training for drug/sex trafficking thereby supplanting low-cost labor from Asia to more local, poor, and in-need areas.

  o Thus significantly improving the living standard for the current lowest-earning population quartile, especially those concentrations in Central America and northern South America.

  o This would undoubtedly Improve Gross Continental Product (GCP=total GNPs) while substantially reducing the incentive/benefit of crime.

- This arrangement will never preclude any mutually <u>beneficial</u> arrangements made with any other Region, Continent, Country, Business or Persons.

  o This, instead of a priority motivated by obligation, guilt, charity, corruption, obscene greed, egomania, power, tax benefits or pressure versus a willing desire to enter into some sort of legitimate, equitable, win-win contract.

  o There would be no prohibition against any charity/philanthropy for those individuals and/or corporations who are on a mission to help those in Africa, Asia, or Europe.

  o Incentives could be used to differentiate those donations made closer to home (more favorable) versus those made farther from home (less favorable). Religious organizations and 'junket'-seekers, please take note!

- It is about time that, every other geographical group be responsible for their own behavior and arrangements without American intervention (I.e., Regime Change/Country Building).

  - Quite simply, we do not **need** it anymore and should no longer **want** it.

  - If any deal makes business sense or political sense or cultural sense or economic sense or even plain ole horse sense believe me, it will happen.

  - Regime Change <u>never</u> will change the hearts, minds, or souls of unwilling participants (E.g., Palestinians).

- We can sell (non-nuclear) weapons limited in range and power to any country that wants to purchase them without various lobbies influencing/preventing the sale one way or the other. Since weapons are our BEST product, this would be our most profitable current balance-of-trade deficit fixer.

  - For example, I think Japan, Taiwan, the Philippines, and South Korea have proven themselves capable of being trusted (maybe even with nuclear?) with their own defense from 1,000 to 3,000-mile away threats.

  - Likewise, if the Middle East has not reached an amical way to co-exist in 2,000 years so, who are we to think WE are ever going to succeed?

  - Let them choose to destroy themselves if they wish as long as <u>no one</u> there can destroy **US**.

  - Ronald Regan's "Star Wars" defense is looking more brilliant as each year passes.

- The Americas seem to have a similar bond formed by exploration, immigration and even the oppression of Indigenous, native-type (Indian?) people.

- There seems much more of a natural potential for identification with and understanding of each other vis-s-vis the other Continents. With apologies to our W.A.S.P. founders. By the way, didn't England really piss off The American Colonies (as well as EVERY one of their other colonies) in the very first place? How did far-reaching geographic expansion work out for them long term? (India; South Africa; Hong Kong). I am still 'rooting' for The Malvinas!

- Seasonal variety (Northern and Southern hemispheres) seems like it could be a beneficial factor for overall development

• It seems unquestionable to me that people's concern for all things in the world radiates outward from themselves in approximate concentric circles. This goes from one's own egotistical self-interests (including family, then friends) of survival all the way to total apathy for those things whom we do not even know exist. If you do not think so, please recollect the various and sundry heartstring-tugging commercials ("Mercy Ship") that attempt to connect us with the previously unconnectable.

- Specifically for example, we care about OUR House MORE than OUR Neighbor's house but OUR Neighborhood more than the neighborhood across the 'tracks.' We care MORE about OUR City than a city 100 miles away in OUR State and OUR State more than a neighboring state. We care MORE about a neighboring State than a state all the way across the Country but OUR Country MORE than a bordering county. We probably care MORE about a bordering Country than a county on the other side of OUR Continent but OUR Continent MORE than a continent across the earth from us. You get the idea how this general concept applies, right?

• If we feel an urgent and perpetual need to tell others how they should live their lives and run their countries, I think we would be much better served to focus diplomacy, money, resources, bribery or, even brute force convincing people in our own Hemisphere.

- ○ Havana and Caracas seem more worthwhile to us than places like Baghdad or Tripoli.

- ○ If I am not mistaken does not Venezuela haven even more oil reserves than Saudi Arabia?

- ○ Does not Cuba have every bit as much potential for greatness as India?

Our Leaders and their constituents have been proceeding with **transactions** and **transitions** for the last century when what is called for is **TRANSFORMATION** in our thinking, in our policies and in our actions. Remember that classic definition of insanity: "Doing the same thing and expecting different results." I am no historian but old enough to see the similarities to our approach with Taliban and the Viet Cong. How did that work out for us? In a word, I see the problem with our Anglo-Saxon/Judeo-Christian approach to the world negotiation is "arrogance." We suffer from myopic vision, short-term planning, and egocentric strategies.

I can remember from grammar school learning of the democracy invented by the Romans to govern their extensive empire. In a time of crisis, they had a system whereby the inevitable gridlock of legislation could be supplanted by what was deemed a "benevolent despot." They were wise enough to realize that, sometimes politics must give way to decisiveness for the common good. I remember Cincinnatus as being one of those benevolent despots who was able to cut through the red tape and lift Rome out of the morass that existed at that time. Rome still fell, however, for being OVER-extended and unable to control itself just like every other empire before and since. Insanity definition anyone? Transformation will probably <u>NOT</u> take place without such a dramatic Constitutional action with lessons learned from past history.

If United Way distributions are allocated by individual choice of charity, then, why can't taxpayers indicate how and where their taxes are spent? That might be a first step in legislators and legislation accurately reflecting the desires of their American 'Bosses.' Can you think of any other situation where the people who pay the price tag do **NOT** get what they want or where the employees do not have to be accountable to their bosses? Maybe Education?????

BIBLICAL BABBLE ON

If Management is already knowing what someone is going to say then, Leadership is NOT finishing their sentence and let them say it anyway.

Firstly, let me give credit where credit is due. The ancient Jewish people were the very first group to create an excellent, one-Godly explanation of how that life on earth came into being. The Old Testament is the "greatest *story* ever told." It is an intellectual masterpiece as far as **fiction** is concerned, primarily considering the time of its writing. Purely ingenious!

Despite all of its wonderful imagination and imagery, there was a tremendous limitation of scope by its writers. They restricted themselves significantly by the smallness of their GEO-centric perspective. Imagine the handicap of knowing less than 1% of the planet and believing that their tangible area in the Middle East was somehow, the **entirety** of creation.

A more crucial error, however, was the extreme limitation of their EGO-centric perspective. I can even understand 'casting' their people in the 'lead' of the story but to dub themselves God's <u>only</u> "chosen" people and relegating the entire rest of the world to "gentile" (not chosen) status was **the** fatal flaw of the writing and THE limitation of their thinking.

The writers were unaware as to how arrogant that would appear and how ridiculous it would seem that A God, THE God, ANY God would grant such a privilege to less than 1% of his or her total (known) human population. To me, Jewish doctrine comes across as those Gentiles, not being kosher, are no more acceptable than 'unclean' shellfish or swine and are not to be co-mingled with any more than meat and dairy. As insulting and offensive as this is, the resulting consequences of this 'classification' seems to result in a long history of Jews losing the 'battles' and losing the 'war.'

To me, this entire 'superiority' objective was a colossal miscalculation of human nature. As much sense as it might have made to the writing committee, they must have suffered from either insular thinking or analysis paralysis. This seemed like a classic case of a solid 'academic' theory failing the experiential, 'wisdom' (eye) test. (They probably should have gotten Solomon more involved on the front end of the strategic verification process). When dealing with other peoples' belief of their own 'truth,' logical thinking and rational argumentation only produces a hypothesis. It seems very naïve to think that the brain's knowledge can prove an experiment test with the feeling in one's heart or the spirit in one's soul.

Despite this myopia and shortsightedness, the Jews had a remarkable opportunity to "revise and resubmit" their tale when one of their own, Jesus Christ, gave them the 'gift' of supernatural editing which, they totally discounted and rejected. Even if one does not believe the whole messiah, savior and resurrection story line, the New Testament still represented a wonderfully fresh sales 'angle' (substituting "love" for legalism) with unlimited marketing opportunities. To my way of believing, the Jews could have dropped the 'exclusivity' niche positioning in favor of a Judeo-Christian 'leadership' niche positioning and made up for any perceived loss of their 'exclusivity' big-time by compensating with the larger 'volume' of BOTH Old **and** New Testament 'followers.' While continually dwelling on "anti-Semiticism," it seems to me that, Jews could be classified as Anti-Gentile for their wholesale 'rejection' of anyone not Jewish. Maybe Sid Roth gets this?

To me, this is the best historical example of a highly intelligent group of individuals acting naive, foolish, ignorant and out-of-touch with overall pragmatic reality. It seems like a highly distorted perspective that expects the world to meet a significant majority of one group's own desires (and not being satisfied nor curtailing substantial 'appetites' despite countless 'rejections') while expecting the rest of the world to willingly settle for much, much less than the 'chosen.' It seems unrealistic to expect the Gentiles to stand by and **not** notice the incredible discrepancies and imbalances of material wealth, political influence, and ideological messaging.

Even more suspect is NOT to remember the long history of similar reactions during century-after-century in culture-after-culture and not acknowledging much validity to any different perspectives at all. By being unwilling to change anything and then blame everyone BUT themselves, it should be no surprise that the "anti-Semitic" response repeats itself over-and-over when there are absolutely no more 'cheeks' left to turn. Already having most of the "eyes for an eye and teeth for a tooth" as it were.

Is this not one, well-accepted definition of "insanity"? You know, doing the exact same thing over-and-over again and expecting DIFFERENT results. Or those who learn "nothing" from history are doomed to REPEAT it? Instead of characterizing "anti-Semitism" as an unfounded, unwarranted prejudice, why not question some of the Jewish leaders (writers of the Old Testament) who decided that Jesus (or any other Gentile for that matter) was NOT worth listening to <u>at all</u>. What if those <u>few</u> leaders at the time of Christ, were in fact wrong or had an ulterior agenda of some kind? Jewish leaders at the time just may have "missed the salvation boat" even though they prophesized a messiah?

With a set of beliefs so much different from the majority of the world (I see an extremely hard line of demarcation between Judeo and Christian, by the way), Jews do not remain to themselves like other distinct groups (E.g., Amish, Mennonites) but rather they expect to play by **their own** 'rules' within the 'system' context of the vast majority. It is as if an American football team went to play in the Canadian Football League but insisted upon having four "downs" to move the ball 10 yards while the rest of the teams had to abide by the process of only three "downs" to make a new first down. Of course, the American team would have a significant advantage. The Canadians, being as polite as they are, might even agree to the difference for a while but eventually, they will become resentful of their 'guests.' Without a homeland until 1948, many (but not all) Jews have behaved like selfish, ungrateful, citizen guests in many countries, never abiding by the parameters of their hosts but rather remaining Jews first and national citizens second.

I remember hearing an extremely cute saying in response to a "born-again" line. "Jesus **saves** but Moses **invests**." We all understand that in general investing produces a better financial return than saving but this represents a nice analogy for a free will choice, NOT a maximized gain. Most seem to want the peace-of-mind safety of 'saving' and are willing to forgo any risk/reward of 'investing' and all of its selling, manipulation, deception, and worldly uncertainty in favor of a more eternal R.O.I.. Maybe a better reaction would be to respect that choice rather than try to exploit its implicit trust and faith. I might even suggest that there is an inverse relationship between wealth and faith (camel through the eye of the needle). At the very least, I think that money can work to erode our need for faith.

I do not think that most Gentile people object at all to the religious freedom of Jews to worship as they wish. After all many Americans, still practice many Judeo-Christion customs and beliefs. The 'rub' seems to be in the area in what many people call "cultural Jews." I do not see this as any kind of religious worship at all. Rather I see this as a human behavior that many people find irritating and take exception to because it extends well beyond an intragroup religious activity and into an inter-cultural dimension within a large majority of society.

We understand that one can <u>always</u> go faster and push harder but most non-Jews do not feel that makes sense within the goals of the overall, infinite plan (I.e., heaven). Most folks do not seem to want other people's 'speed' and 'force' to upset any natural pace and equilibrium of the total spiritual dynamic for the vast majority. I would think that the Jews would be thrilled that so many people of the world follow the word of one of 'their own.' It is the Gospel (Jesus' teachings) and not the Talmud/Torah, however. Personally, I think "Jews for Jesus" (Messianic Jews) is the way to go to have the best of both worlds.

I feel that if American Jews pursue the same path of substantial control and significant manipulation (E.g., The Media) they are on then, the tolerance will eventually end, as it always has. As Joe Biden said, the Jewish people have the most impact on American culture (E.g., at one time: 22% of Supreme Court vs. 2% of population) of any one group over the last generation. The question is: do most people **like** the direction that impact is heading towards? (Ultra Progressive hard Left turn towards Socialism/Communism?).

You see, research data can negate the emotional argument of Anti-Semitism. I think I read that, one-half of all Billionaires in American are Jewish. I read that 50% of all Jews in the United States are millionaires. Or look at the dominance of professional sports team ownership if you want? This is not an unfounded stereotype here but only plain socio-economic demographic information. As such, it seems to present quite a disproportionate and unbalanced scenario. If true and continuing then, the American 'Jew Jitsu' of 'grappling' with so much money and power may not end well… once again. But, it does NOT have to!

That direction seems to be moving us increasingly towards 'tangible' measurements of life's purpose at the expense of those 'intangible' measures. We acknowledge that worldly goal attainment is most definitely in the Jewish "wheelhouse." Nevertheless, for those who think that the "intangibles" are a far superior value indicator, the tendency is to dismiss those tangible measures until we start choking on them and then what usually follows is social 'vomit' directed at those purveyors of the tangible.

Quite simply, the majority of people do not use the tangibles of facts, data, and information as the scoring system of a human's worth. I do not believe that humans are supposed to know **everything** because that is what separates us from our Creator. Knowing too much (vis-à-vis TRUST/FAITH) can only lead to trouble as we misinterpret the intentions, or its consequences as 'mapped' by the Creator. Does anyone remember the parable lesson of eating fruit from the Tree of Knowledge? (again, written by the Jewish Old Testament writers). I guess they pick & choose what is valid or not?

Many Jews have proudly stated and acted as if, they are "right," and the entire world is "wrong." That has never been, is not now and I suspect, never will be a palatable situation for most non-Jews. It might even be possible in the short term or for a specific issue but in the end for overall living, the majority always get their way. The difference now is that the

Jewish-Americans can always take their ideology to the state of Israel to live and practice Judaism to one's heart content. Even that, however, causes incredible Middle East dissention impacting upon the rest of the World.

I often wonder why the Palestinians have paid the price for the Holocaust brought about by Germany. Aren't Palestinians Semitic also? Shouldn't the State of Israel have been carved out of prime German land as a reparation for the atrocities? I just wonder if their past successes of capitalizing upon **their** values/beliefs/behaviors as a small minority in largely Gentile populations would replicate in a homeland state where there are majority Jews and a minority Gentiles. Who would exploit whom? West Bank anyone?

By the way, this is not Anti-Semitic as much as it is Pro-Gentilic! The Italians are often competitive with the Jews and in some ways repel each other due to similarities (E.g., importance of families). Why is there not an anti-Roman phenomenon of such pronounced discrimination? I have anecdotally noticed a remarkably similar trajectory of Indian immigrants to that of the Jewish immigration, especially in terms of educational/entrepreneurial achievement and accomplishment. Why is there not worldwide prejudicial treatment against them?

I'm just suggesting that it may be time for Jewish Leadership to take **'partial' responsibility for the concept of Anti-Semitic "defamation"** and change something/anything to avoid it reaching any of the horrific consequences of the past. Just modifying Orthodox to "Conservative" and "Reform" is not enough realization.

Maybe if they had a single-voice 'spokesperson'-type like the Catholics have the Pope, things could be 'modified' as life in the world changes over time. I remember how the meatless Friday guide was changed after it no longer made sense for the modern world. Controversial yes but at the same time helpful.

RANDOM FOCUS

If Management is being annoyed that a bicycle rider in the rain
slows down your car's progress in traffic then,
Leadership is making sure that you do not
splash him/her as you pass the bicycle.

- All is fair in love and war…and Politics…and Business…and Entertainment…and Sports…apparently?

- The world has ALWAYS been going to "Hell in a Handbasket."

…it is just a different basket!

- Dementia…maybe we have just lived too long, thought too much, and overcrowded our heads with too much useless, unsort-able quantity of information?

- Is Height (lack of it) the American discrimination prejudice that no one is willing to talk about…yet?

- Corporate Executive Compensation- you make a bunch when you perform and you put half in escrow so, if you DO NOT perform later, you pay some back! Athletes? Entertainers?

- Romance and Religion are terribly similar. A lot of money is being made by selling unrealistic, unattainable fantasies through exploitation of people's hopes and dreams. The fable of 'easy' perfection does not exist and to turn people's faith and trust of the unknown into a commodity is despicable. This creates DEPENDANCY on other things outside of and other than OURSELVES.

- In order to get our United States citizen I.D., how about having to sign a sworn statement to swear unconditional allegiance to American interests and not to possess any 'assault' weaponry?

- Can someone please tell me the difference between saying that: one's white skin color (race) is supreme/superior **OR** that one's Jewish religion (race) is for God's ONLY (supreme/superior) "chosen" people?

- Where does the line end between the Human Nature need for Women to be sexually attractive to Men and Men to be sexually attracted to Women (for procreation) end and "Impropriety/Harassment" begin? That line always darts around mercurially and 5% of all People will always miss it, no matter what.

- A.rtificial I.ntelligence, the new messiah? Or THE new Satan?

- The Protestant Reformation is the biggest Self-Rationalization in history.

- Human Nature is an anvil hanging from the Divine Nature parachute.

- A Judeo-Christian foundation? Jews want to excel during their lifetime on earth and Christians want to excel during eternity in the afterlife.

- Everyone is trying to make a huge deal about the tiny differences between their (no two are alike) particular life's 'snowflake.' Yet, no one seems to realize that as a race, modern life is burying us under 'snowdrifts' and we need to just focus on uniting to shovel ourselves out from under.

- Should not the term be "diff-ability" not "dis-ability"?

- For desirable locations, wouldn't a better term be "SUP-urbs" rather than "SUB-urbs"?

- A Leader needs an organization whose purpose is that which he/she can be passionate about… A manager only needs an organization that will provide a paycheck.

- The United States is like that 'easy' girl in high school/college with whom everyone wants to have-their-'way' then move on, as opposed to the 'commitment-demanding' woman with whom they eventually marry…like Denmark?

- If someone were **really and truly** convinced of one's own Religion's 'after-life' promise, why would they ever have to harm another individual in the least for any 'different' after-life plan beliefs? They would be too confident and secure to give a damn.

- America is most like a multi-level marketing scheme; one always needs new immigrants "downstream' to keep it going. The problem is that, at some point it has to end because all the 'lines' eventually get all dried up!

- While we tend to think that "it is better to give than receive;" the truth is that "givers" would be pretty unfulfilled if there were no "takers." Both are necessary to complete their equation, and neither is more noble or less noble than the other.

- The words "hero" (as opposed to doing his/her job), "expert" (as opposed to the answer *du jour*), "family" (blood is STILL thicker than water), and the artificially constructed "attractive," (as opposed to the more 'natural' terms "pretty"/"handsome" and the indisputably subjective "beautiful") are really getting overused these days and therefore, tremendously diminished in importance. These have become the 'participation' trophies of the modern vernacular.

- When did advertisers discover that everyone "deserves" or are "entitled" to something that they are NOT getting?

- Is "just coffee" between a man and a woman ever completely 'innocent'?

- Am I the only one that laughs ironically at any low-to-the-ground sports car **legally** parked in a "Handicapped" spot?

- Why haven't all of the "brown" M & M's been replaced by "purple" ones making all of the 6 colors either primary or secondary? After all, they are ALL "brown" on the inside, aren't they?

- Maybe Men would not be so afraid of marriage if it were called "Settling Up" instead of "Settling Down"?

- As important as "First Impressions" are, my experience is that "LAST Impressions" have had much more impact on my life!

- Anytime a NEW XMAS song comes out, anyone can "cover" it for the next 5 years then, a moratorium on cover versions should exist for the next 25 years. This moratorium should be retroactive in order to 'grandfather' all of the traditional "classics" from being abused via sheer unnecessary repetition.

- The "commercialization" of Christmas will not go away so, I make no argument against it. Rather, I suggest a modification that might be better for GIFT receivers (especially children), but maybe NOT for the toy companies. All of the lights, decorations, songs, etc. can all go on as presently, but I propose the gifting take place with one gift on the 25th (not HIS real birthday anyway) of each month for the entire year (I.e., 12 gifts). Kind of like Chanukah on steroids! It is impossible to appreciate so many gifts at one time (all that wasted wrapping) and since I am too realistic to think that the number of gifts will ever decrease. At least by spreading them out over 12 months it will give more thought/appreciation to everything connected with the "reason for the season". As it exists now, we are just making things easier for the toy makers, gift distributors and gift sellers…screw them!

- How can anyone know what name to give a newborn which best reflects the person he/she is? I propose a "working" (draft) name until some age (10, 12, 13?) when an appropriate (and permanent) name can be chosen to best reflect a person's true personality/image/character, etc. Get over it Social Security Number Bureaucrats!

- How come a coach does not have to honor their contract when they get a better offer BUT his/her employer has to continue to pay for the duration of the contract when they are fired? Sports Broadcasting commenting jobs notwithstanding.

- "Virtual" ANYTHING compared to the "real" thing is like masturbation is compared to sex; better than nothing but leaving much to be desired unless you prefer alone-ness?

- "Chronological" Age is such a restrictive measure of longevity compared to "Biological" Age much the same way that "skin-deep beauty" is a limited measure of 'inner' Human Value.

- The downside of a country with "Free Speech" is that the average citizen is *tsunami-ed* with too many words strung together into "opinionated" ideas/concepts. 10% of all of them are essential, indisputable truths (to any specific individual) and 10% of them are totally useless opinions. That 20% is not the problem. It is 80% that might be useful, plausible, viable, important (to any particular individual) BUT dominates all of our thoughts, confuses the hell out of us, causes questions of self-doubt and is a less optimal use, (if not a total waste) of our precious time.

- It seems to me that, if you do NOT like something or someone, then everything they do will seem exactly and dreadfully SIMILIAR. Yet, if you LIKE what they do, then everything they do will seem totally and delightfully DIFFERENT. A recording artist or an actor, for example. It is merely a personal choice as to whether you only superficially examine the similarities or take the time/effort to experience the deeper distinctions.

- I do not mind the exercise of Power unless it is extremely DIS-proportionate. For Example, it one group represents 2% of the total population yet controls 30% of the total wealth, I am concerned. Or, if a specific group represents 20% of the total population yet comprises 80% of the political power representation, I am worried. Conversely, if any particular group makes up 50% of a complete universe yet ONLY possesses 10% of decision-making, I am (currently) scared!

- What is WRONG with me? When I see a racoon roadkill, I am sad. When I see opossum roadkill, I am not at all sad. Makes me think about how difficult life must be for ugly people and so easy for the "cute."

- Do not emphasize having a Gender Identity, an Ethnic Identity, or a Racial Identity as much as striving to be a HUMAN BEING.

- Do not identify as much with any one Religious denomination as much as identify with being a "Child of God."

- National boundaries are so arbitrary why not instead become a citizen of the Universe or at least of the Earth?

- I always feel bad for a woman who wants to "identify" as male (in dress, hair, etc.) when 'she' has big breasts. It just ruins the entire look.

- In the debate over the 'best' gender, one only needs to look at the 'components' of reproduction. **One** of a woman's lifetime total of 30-35 eggs can routinely sell for $25,000-$50,000 (plus "expenses") to an infertile couple. On the other hand, a **billion** of a man's potential DAILY egg-penetrating 'swimmers' will net the donor for around $100 at the local sperm bank.

  - Since the female is clearly the most important/valuable gender, my thought is that "men" invent 'muscular' things like sports, business, and war to compensate for their inferior contribution to life's most incredible Human 'trick'…creating life *in utero*.

- Here is a suggestion that makes too much sense to ever be considered— move Thanksgiving to the last Thursday in OCTOBER. We do not need to wait until November anymore for food to be harvested. It would provide a perfect mid-point break for EVERYONE'S fall school semester (between start-of-school and Holiday/winter break in order to facilitate vacations for the entire family). Finally, it would not 'crowd' upon the Christmas season (and ANOTHER turkey dinner) so much. Like I said, snowball's chance in Hell!

- Labeling the color of people as either "black" and/or "white," aside from being incredibly IN-accurate, sets up humans for diametrically (polar opposite) opposed segregation. If we were all just various shades in between brown and beige, not only would we be a part of the SAME color spectrum, but it would also more accurately reflect the similarities of our humanity BENEATH the mere superficiality of skin. Surely this would connect us to those more important, deeper, and more meaningful factors that God must have intended.

- How about we simply identify all people as "V" if they are born with a vagina and "P" if they are born with a penis? After that, anyone can look/act any damn well they please.

- How about EACH sport (Scholastic and Collegiate) team (at EVERY level) be divided into **only** "Varsity" for the best available players and the "Junior Varsity" for those who do <u>not make</u> the varsity regardless of GENDER (or age).

- With all of the Covid Pandemic symptomatic treatments going on, the proverbial Tail is wagging the perpetual Dog. The emphasis should have been and should be going forward is Personal Responsibility for Individual IMMUNITY (like taking Vitamin D-3 for example). Virtually no support (education, healthcare, insurance benefits, nutritional's) is given to PREVENTING and RESISTING ANY virus that comes down the 'pike.' We can never control any and all of the "external" situations which come our way; ONLY our own response (not reaction) to them. Let us not put the Cart in front of the Horse, please! Oh, that's right, Big Pharma and the Governments sell 'Carts.'

- The thing that bugs me the most about the United States and its Judeo-Christian/Anglo-Saxon foundation is that it is based on and relies on the principle of the Predator/Prey concept. I know all of you Darwinists out there think I have proven your point about the 'jungle' "laws of nature." That is fine if you want to limit our potential to the Human "Animal" level. I, on the other hand, am just delusional enough to wish, hope and pray for more enlightenment. Since animals never kill for 'sport' or take more than they need, I wonder how we should explain why 'powerful' and greedy People will choose to get excessively rich through exploiting others by selling things like lottery tickets; drugs; nicotine; alcohol; caffeine, excessive salt & sugar; depreciating materialism; unrealistic romance; and tithed salvation?

  - -Here's how? Powerful people 'EXPLOIT' rather than 'ADVOCATE' Human Nature. They understand that the 'average' person has no time, interest and/or ability to read all of the **"fine print"** of life. For example: legislative details; electronic 'inserts;' package/

product labeling; media 'fact' checking; explicit/implicit contract language. Other rich people pay lawyers to read for them while the rest of us gullible and naïve must trust in and rely on those few 'advocators' of our welfare.

- Anything REAL is always better than anything ARTIFICIAL, regardless what the Food Industry says.

- I am not a vegetarian, but I do take Umbridge to the sight of eating establishments with deliriously happy depictions of chickens, cattle, turkeys and especially pigs (at BBQ's) when they are just about to be eaten.

- If you ever wonder how resistant people are to change even when learning has advanced, just look to the 5-pointed illustrations of "stars" even though, they are ROUND! Close second are the drawings of human hearts which look like nothing like the real things. Thanks to Hallmark and Saint Valentine.

- If we call Television TV, then why is not the Telephone TP?

- What makes fires suspicious? Do they just NOT TRUST anything?

- Do Clothes REALLY make the man? When you define life so superficially, don't be surprised if you get yourself a heavy-drinking, constantly womanizing, gambling man whose morality is self-serving, fidelity is fleeting, ethics are situational, and values are incredibly shallow.

- Analogous lesson for men who are obsessed with big breasted women. Guys, breasts are for BABIES…time to re-examine your own adult maturity level?

- Here is what I have learned from **other** people so far…
  - from the Italians: When it is Heart vs. Head, the Heart ALWAYS wins.
  - from the Japanese: The Older someone's Age, the more Respect is earned/deserved.
  - from the Greeks: You cannot really have a Great time without breaking a few dishes.

- from the Koreans: Your body's 'inside' health is more important than your body's 'outside' fragrance.

- from the Chinese: One's actions have impact beyond one's own lifetime and should be measured by such.

- from the Irish: Laughter is essential to Life and Alcohol is essential to Laughter.

- from the English: Do not ever think that one deserves to take more than one's FAIR share of the world's "oyster" resources.

- from the Spanish: Let the French **think** they have the best Cuisine, they **know** for sure that they do.

- from the Scandinavians: Any Society's 'chain' is only as strong (I.e., "balanced") as its weakest (person's) 'link.'

- from the Russians: those who do not learn from history…are just DOOMED!

- from the Germans: It is good to be Accurate and Precise.

- from the Canadians: Get over Yourself and just "Chill."

- from the Mexicans: Tomorrow will almost always be a Better Day.

- from the Brazilians: Love of Life is not circumstantial; it is one's own CHOICE.

- from the French: It is good to think highly of yourself…just not TOO highly.

- from the Swiss: there are very few things that are worth fighting over instead of negotiating for.

- from the Jews: if the entire rest of the world disagrees, maybe think about Re-considering any self-written historical position of "chosen" favor.

- from my fellow Americans: cultural facts have absolutely no relationship to one's individual truths. The U.S.A.'s cultural 'gears' are lubricated with pure, unadulterated bullshit.

WHAT'S A META FOR?

If Management is calling "Shotgun" first when riding in a car then, Leadership is suggesting that the person with the longest legs sit up front.

Sometimes, the best way to fully communicate a multifaceted idea to a diverse group of individuals is to utilize analogy or metaphor. When it comes to a complicated concept like Leadership, I thought most people could relate to its comparison to driving. Most everyone drives as soon as they are qualified and similarly, most people start telling others what to do about the time they learn to talk. See if you can draw your own connections to your idea of Leadership? So, here goes…

…Driving is a job (paying attention, focusing, and concentrating), and it is the only one I know of where everyone is treated exactly equal regardless of "competence" (E.g., reflexes, peripheral vision, reaction timing, distance judgment, etc.) level. It is also seldom ever re-tested after issuance. Automobile licenses all have the same rights and responsibilities yet, the impact on others (I.e., "followers") can be quite different experiences. **<u>HINT</u>: Many accidents are caused by OVER-correcting or OVER-reacting to current circumstances instead of seeing and responding accurately to the REAL situation. For example:**

- Don't you love a driver who remains in the left lane directly alongside another driver in the right lane for mile-after-mile? One who is either unwilling/unable to speed up sufficiently in order to pass OR slow down enough in order to let others pass. I am not sure if this is that driver's only opportunity to exhibit any 'power' in his/her life or he/she is just terrified to be behind the wheel of a moving vehicle. In any event, it BLOCKS anyone who chooses to travel at a different rate of speed.

- What about the person who remains in a right lane (as opposed to the center lane) when going straight even though a right turn is permitted? This person seems totally clueless to other drivers behind who might have a different route/schedule needed or he/she cannot handle the 'intricate' planning required for their right turn coming within the next mile.

- How about just taking one's foot OFF of the accelerator FIRST when one needs to slow down (seeing a light change up ahead) rather than ALWAYS braking immediately?

- Let alone the 'clueless' driver who is first in line at a red light and does NOT seem to understand that "green" ALWAYS follows "red" (except in parts of Europe where they seem smart enough to 'warn' idiots with a "yellow" in-between). Knowing that he/she will get through the light change (while texting, eating, or doing makeup) but yet is oblivious to others behind who might NOT make it through due to a tortoise-walking-through-molasses 'reaction' reflex response. Others behind might have a life 'agenda' issue that may require more time-saving at that time

- If I were to hazard a guess, I would state that going too slow (especially when turning) is every bit as dangerous as going too fast…especially when the reason is texting. When are we going to have an organization named MATT- Mothers Against Terrifying Texting?

- When making a left turn, why not move as far left and as far forward as possible (into the intersection) so, as NOT to make right-turners and/or straight-goers have to wait unnecessarily? Signaling in general has become a lost courtesy.

- I love the 'one-speed-only' drivers who cannot/will not speed up or slow down just a little depending on the situation. For example, to compensate for someone trying in the oncoming lane to enter a traffic flow from a perpendicular turn.

- Are people intentionally and deceptively "sneaky" or just stupid when they do not turn on their "left turn signal" indicator until you get right behind them at a light and have no other option but to wait unnecessarily? Signaling sems to be a symbol of 'power' for some drivers.

- When people do not know the laws (like who goes first at a four-way stop when simultaneously arriving), they seem to opt for either: scared polite or annoyed aggressive.

- I used to think that the world was divided into those people who thought that a 'yellow' light means "hurry up and go" OR "hurry up and stop." Now I think that, IF I am alone it means: "hurry up and go" BUT If I have my kids in the car it means "hurry up and stop." Also, people have shifted from running through yellow lights to running through red lights much more often.

- Tailgating has seemed to have gotten much worse lately regardless of any speed the front car is going. Also, the willingness to flash one's light and/or beep one's horn has increased even outside of big cities.

- Aggression has taken on a new level of intensity. Beyond the "road rage" figure pointing and inaudible cursing, people now seem willing to use their autos like bumper cars at an amusement park.

A "NEW" INTELLIGENCE?

*If Management is picking out all of your favorite items
from one 'dish' at the buffet then,
Leadership is being 'grateful' and liking whatever comes out in each ladle.*

For a long time, we have used I. Q. (Intelligence Quotient) as a measure of an individual's worth to society. The problem is the people who developed the instrument only considered and measured a rather narrow view of word (English) and number (Math) mastery. Governed by the WASP-influenced E.T.S. in Princeton, New Jersey.

Out of the Multiple Intelligences (like 8 kinds) research, some people added the concept of E. Q. (Emotional Intelligence Quotient), as a better indicator of one's potential for success in the modern world. The limitation I see with only considering INTER-personal and INTRA-personal faculties is that they can become highly individualized and subject to 'sins' of the ego like delusion, manipulation, generalization, justification, and rationalization.

With the ongoing stalemate battles among legal, ethical, and moral issues, I am wondering if we need leadership by people who can use more than just their head and their heart. I am proposing a new measure for the future that might factor in the qualities of the "soul." Not religion mind you, that factor can remain in the purview of war and the reasons for killing.

I am talking about something called S. Q. (Spiritual Intelligence Quotient); an indicator that goes beyond the reason and logic of tangible resources. A measure of humanity which assumes any Creator would judge which is "right or wrong" against a period of eternity.

<u>S. Q.</u> =

The Golden Rule + a Genuine Fear of God/Judgment Day + Sincere Humility + the Courage to Defend Moral Principles + Total Respect for Everyone and Everything + a Healthy Dose of Shame for Wrongdoing + a Holistic Ethical Perspective + Genuine Comprehension of the Long-Term Consequences + Strong Sincere Faith + Authentic Trust + Agility + Flexibility + Adaptability + Versatility + Creativity+ A Genuine Live and Let Live Philosophy Because "To Each His/her Own".

<u>Minus</u>

Arrogance + Ego + Self-Righteousness + Self-Importance + Entitlement + Selfishness + Myopia + Manipulative Actions + Deceitfulness + 'Deservence' + Hubris + Delusions of Grandeur

TAXING SKULL CRAMPS

*If Management is 'scope' shooting your deer limit at a corn
'feed' while sitting in your deer stand then,
Leadership is tracking a buck for hours and felling him
with just one heart hit from your bow and arrow.*

If this country really wants to make some changes that place "America First," how about these:

1. <u>Charitable Deductions</u>- Why not provide more favorable tax deduction rates for those philanthropic contributions that directly benefit The United States and less favorable rates for those that benefit foreign countries?

2. <u>Religious Efforts</u>- Why not provide different (higher) tax deduction rates for those expenses that are directly connected to helping other (less fortunate) American citizens and a lower tax deduction rate (or limits) for other, potentially inflated expenses such as "operations" or bogus "mission" trips?

3. <u>Other Non-Profits</u>- Why not regulate all Non-Profit organizations (even schools and hospitals) to close 'loopholes' which provide unfair competition with similar institutions. This, to ensure that their missions are in fact, doing the work of 'giving' to those in need and not going to things like discretionary capital expansions. Let's level the 'playing field' for Non-Profits who sell the same products/services for **less** that For-Profits because they are not paying taxes on them while tax payers subsidize them.

4. **Internal Revenue Information Technology**- Most importantly, it would be incredibly valuable (and downright terrifying) to our

governments, if American taxpayers were able to indicate on tax return forms, individual preferences (by percentages) of revenue to be spent on various budget categories (E.g., defense, healthcare, environment, philanthropy, etc.). In addition to legislators knowing the real desires of their constituents, it would make for a great 'scorecard' come re-election time. This should neutralize much of the self-serving influence of most lobbyists and political action committees. Kind of what the United Way does for its donors.

OH! PINIONS

If Management is putting everything away so
YOU can find them then, Leadership is putting things in a place
where anyone who needs them can easily find them.

Like they say about "hit" songs, they kinda write themselves in a pretty brief time.

That is exactly what I believe is WRONG with America these days… over complicating things by desperate people using purely intellectual arguments *ad nausem* to justify their actions while being completely blind themselves to the bigger simplicity of truth.

The real dilemma is that Politics is a "short-term" activity while the REAL problems of the world take "long-term" solutions. Global Warming (or any facsimile thereof) takes a 50-year plan with 'benchmarks' to be targeted and hit every 5 years in order to evaluate, modify and revise. The Budget Deficit needs to be addressed IMMEDIATELY with specific 'sacrifices' made by ALL in order to begin to get a 'handle' on multiple solutions in order to address a problem which will take 25 years to fix. The Middle East has been a "fluster cluck" throughout recorded history and it seems totally delusional to anyone who thinks it will get solved during anyone's political term. As long as politicians are obsessed with getting elected, none of the real problems of America (and the world) will ever change until the proverbial "fit" hits the perennial "shan."

The United States of America is just ONE country in the world but one with a unique culture all its own. As such, anyone who wants to live here needs to accept its rules, regulations, policies, and procedures or find a county that is better suited for them. In business, the overriding determining factor in career success is the "person-job 'fit'". Likewise, successful citizenship can be best determined by the person-culture "fit." If there is **not** a good match, it is destined to be a long, painful, and unsuccessful endeavor for both any individual AND society at large.

I am not even saying that America is the only and/or best place to live BUT if one is going to live here then, understand the environment, accept it, and make it work the best you can. In my Italian family's case, there was much about this 200-year-old history that seemed inferior to our 2,000-year old one. Since Italians have long been identified as the "least assimilable" of all the European immigrants, if we can do it, I would think any group can. Every immigrant group 'huddles' together in neighborhoods but it should be for the purpose of helping each other adjust to the "American" way of life and should not be to create terrorist 'cells' in order to tear down what already exists most successfully.

My grandfather thought that the Italian language was much more beautiful than English, but we all learned to speak English immediately. I was named after him, but his name was Giuseppe, and my American birth certificate says "Joseph." He felt that American food was incredibly substandard to Italian food, but we learned to cook "American" and eat "fast food." Compared to Italian fashion, American clothes were inferior, but we dressed to fit in. American automobiles were ugly compared to those from Milan, but we drove what everyone else was driving. He believed Art and Music from the "Old Country" was Classical and American Arts were nothing more than fleeting "pop," but we listened to Elvis and looked at Warhol.

The simple point being when NOT in Rome, do NOT even try to do what the Romans do and so, we accepted the "pros" of the U.S. (more opportunities) with the "cons" (adolescent civilization versus mature/wise one). Therein lies the current dilemma America faces. Like it or not, the White, Anglo-Saxon, Protestant Males founded this country and as such, got to write up the rules/laws (I.e., Constitution, Bill-of-Rights, Principles, Policies, Amendments, Definitions of "Intelligence," "Beauty," "Hard Work," "Values," "Ethics," etc.). Are they perfect? Nope!

The point is, as imperfect as it is, there is definitely **"AN AMERICAN WAY OF LIFE."** If you don't accept/like/live it then, do not participate in "throwing out the baby with the bathwater." Either help to make it better or find a more suitable way of life somewhere else....PERIOD.

Could the Founders have anticipated everything three hundred years into the future where muscats became AR-15's? When Freedom of "Christian" Denominations became Hindu, Muslim and Buddhist religious choices? How "all men created equal" became self-identifying gender selection? Would Freedom of Speech ever be suppressed by Freedom of the Press? Can they be 'expanded' within the basic 'framework' of that which is The United States of America (Constitutional Amendments?) Certainty! But as defined by the "moral majority" and NOT the "minority tyranny" exceptions. I.e., the <u>adaptation</u> burden is on the MINORITY.

How about considering an Amendment that, "All Federal Judges being appointed by and answer/report to the Supreme Court?" That would eliminate the politicalization of Executive Branch appointees who feel pressured/obligated to judge not 'blindly' but become "weaponized."

I can live with a lot of variety and diversity but NOT at the expense of the American Dream. The economic system of Capitalism (even with a few Socialistic overtones) cannot be undermined in favor of anything that even hints of Marxism/Communism. The Democratic features of our Constitutional Republic cannot even entertain any features of Elite Totalitarianism. The humility of a God-fearing nature (E.g., the teaching of Jesus Christ, the Man) is essential regardless of which God is followed. Any person or group that thinks so is in the wrong place and needs to find a country that is a better 'fit.' It is not so different, really, it is just like changing jobs. That goes for the new immigrants as well as the folks who have been here for generations. F.Y.I. - Scandinavian counties exceed America in many critical life categories!

So, in a "Keep It Simple Stupid" (K.I.S.S.) 'nutshell,' here is what is necessary to become a successful American citizen (AND IT HAS AB-

SOLUTELY NOTHING TO DO WITH AGE, GENDER, RACE, RELIGION, ETHNICITY, etc.):

- Believe in some Supreme Creator that will judge your soul at some point.

  - this, in order to have a **basic but strong moral and ethical basis** and a healthy dose of **shame** when needed. Things like Trust, Respect, Humility and Kindness are Universal.

- Keep Government(s) at a **minimal level** of necessary involvement!

  - **protecting/defending** its citizens from ANY harm through **<u>LAWS</u>** (both written and unwritten) is the **main priority**. Also, advocating for only those **truly less fortunate** with an actual, ability-to-be-demonstrated 'need.'

- Make your concept of **"Family" the foundational structure** of your relationships.

- Take the 'best' job you can (no matter how menial) and **do it as well as you can**. Then continue moving **"up the 'ladder'"** no matter how demanding it is.

- **Save** as much money as you can by living BELOW your means (in order to 'free' oneself from the vicissitudes of the Economy) at all times.

- Take those savings and **invest** them in things which provide the **best "return"** (things like education, health, and a home for said family), NOT Depreciating assets!

- The "goal" must always be that each succeeding generation has it **'better'** off than the previous one thereby 'resisting' the strong temptations satisfy the 'world' NOW with your debt.

- Allegiance must always be to **America FIRST** and country-of-origin, second. (E.g., **English** must be the first preferred, national language).

- Look for opportunities to **serve** your neighborhood, community, state, and county whenever possible.

- **Vote** for the representative(s) that best serve America's interests. It is perfectly fine to start out as more liberal for progress and gradually become more conservative as you have more "wealth" at 'stake.'

- As a **"Land of Laws,"** it is always best (for the Common Good) to abide by all laws/policies/procedures/rules/regulations and **support** those who enforce ALL of these even if you do not agree 100% of the time.

- Do not ever confuse **opinions** (data, information, facts, knowledge) with one's individual and "wise" TRUTH.

- **And FINALLY, any and all Politicians and Media "talking heads" must be hooked up to a "Lie Detector," visible to the viewing audience, when speaking to the tax-paying constituents.**

Bottom line here is that America needs a specific, formal, and officially legal set of Immigration laws that serve both its current and future <u>legal</u> citizens FIRST and FOREMOST!

ECLECTIC CONSISTENCY

(OR THINGS THAT I HAVE LEARNED THE 'HARD' WAY BUT HAVE NOT YET MASTERED)

If Management is seeing a person who cannot afford their 'lifestyle' and thinks, "How Foolish?" then, Leadership is asking, "How can I help increase this person's self-worth?"

The World likes to separate every individual from his or her own harmonious balance (for the World's own benefit). That is to say that the World likes to view people primarily as <u>either</u> only Physical, Intellectual, Emotional <u>or</u> Spiritual beings. When, in fact, what is best for each person is to utilize those 4 components proportionately to synergize themselves for the most 'leverage' (think martial arts) possible. It is not the separation of those 4 aspects that makes us our "best" but rather it is the connecting and combining of the 4 that gives us our healthiest and happiest dimension.

- For example, Sports, Entertainment and Military seem preoccupied with young peoples' **Physical** strength, speed, beauty, or talent to the exclusion of a well-rounded approach.

- The Academic world only seems to value and care about one's 'peak' **Intellectual** brainpower used disproportionately vis-a-vis the other 3.

- Social Media play havoc with peoples' **Emotions** to the point of pathological consequences.

- Organized Religion plays heavy-handed with our 'hypothetical' **Spiritual** salvation outcome at the expense of one's whole being.

At the risk of "oversimplification," the one thing that I would recommend is that everyone look inside themselves to see what (un-balanced) disconnections exist within and where/how those 4 facets can be Better

Connected or RE-Connected. That may explain a lot of one's own dissatisfaction with or underutilization of oneself, IF there is any?

IF the above-mentioned 4 things are NOT in balance, bad/weird things can happen…NOT devastating things mind you…just less-than optimal. Think of the Bell Curve where too much of anything can be just as bad (if not worse) as too little of that very **same** thing. I am thinking about being told as a youngster that, "you are too smart for your own good." WHAT! How can being too smart (or too rich/thin for that matter) EVER be bad? Glad you asked. If, for example, one is so smart about creating "rationalizations" then, one might be substituting a logical explanation for emotions when an emotional response is warranted. Therefore, one is "thinking" (because it is easier for them) when "feeling"(but avoided) is required. For years, I really, REALLY thought I was describing <u>feelings</u> in therapy when in reality, I was only describing <u>thoughts</u>. Until I realized the differences and how to use them, I never changed (I.e., became "better") and even more significantly, I was clueless about what I was missing and/or falsely replacing.

I have found that, in almost all instances, "low and slow" is the best way to proceed with things. In a world where bigger is purportedly better and faster gets all the notoriety, most important things lose their 'taste' or worse, even get 'burned' when rushed. Whether exercising, cooking or even interacting, a gradual warm/build-up followed by peak performance and then finished with a cool-down period seems to enable us to treat important things in life with the best, gentle care. This, as opposed, to the more common 'wheel spinning' and the frantic starting/stopping of the chronic "hurry up and wait."

ॐ likewise, the most valuable things in life cannot be made up for in 'bulk.' One cannot binge on sleep, exercise, nutrition, watching, time, communication, etc. and expect to replace the qualitative factors gained by consistent, slow, and steady doses of life's most worthwhile 'inputs'. They directly affect our 'outputs.'

I do not think that "Givers" are any more noble than "Takers." Givers, in their own selfishness, need Takers in order to complete the chosen 'cycle' in their life. If, it is in fact, it is "BETTER to give than receive" then the Takers are necessary to complete the 'equation' for the Givers that would be impossible without them. I do agree that, once one learns the 'rush' of satisfaction from giving, it is easy to get addicted to it. However, do not resent the takers because without them, one gets no 'rush.' AND that 'rush' is usually better than whatever has been taken.

Unless one is going to have an infinite, never-ending relationship with someone then, I think that "last" impressions are even more important than "first" impressions. So often relationships which end on a bad and sour note actually have much more time and feelings invested **after** the relationship has ended vis-a-vis the entire length of time **during** that relationship. Yet, truly little care goes into how we want to be "remembered" compared to initially working our first (artificially generated?) impressions of the job, friendship, romance, family, etc.

In our need to pursue any great "perfection" (either imposed by the World or by ourselves) in life, we often are blind to the many 'goods' along the way. Since we are conditioned to believe that we all are entitled to the 'best,' we do not realize that the accumulation of many 'goods' in life usually add up to much more than the ONE 'best' that we usually <u>never</u> get (E.g., lotteries). Many people and institutions benefit along the way of everyone's perfection pursuit so, there is not as much support to encourage collection of the 'goods' and many of us miss out on so much. Furthermore, we can easily be forced to settle for **less** overall than if we had an accurate value of all the little 'goods' which can really add up. In a word, try not to let the <u>potential</u> **great** get in the way of the <u>actual</u> **goods**. In reality, the best that most of us can do is "good" anyway so why let our own ego (shaped by the media and others) make us think that we somehow deserve more than that?

Despite all the movies, romance novels or Disney products, "love' is not some magical, mystical thing that befalls us from on 'high' IF we are lucky enough and conform to a whole set of prescribed, commercial behaviors. For example, like the clothes we wear, the car we drive, the way we look, the school we attend, our church, our job, etc. Love is a choice that we make, pure and simple. The world makes the most money selling Romantic Love but the greatest love of all is selfless, *agape* Love. An unconditional Love of our self, an intimate partner, our family, our friends or just mankind in general totally trumps any of the *quid pro quo* conditional 'deals' that we make in the pursuit of more shallow, superficial relationships masquerading as 'love.'

Speaking of real Love, it involves a level of <u>Risk</u> which most people are unable and/or unwilling to take. Most of us want predictable outcomes BEFORE investing ourselves in any relationship but Love just does not work that way...sorry! Why should life's best Reward come easy and to those devoid of courage? Rollo May, in his book <u>Love and Will</u>, states that the opposite of Love is <u>not</u> Hate but Apathy. I think he means that, apathy is an easy way out for most people but caring enough to engage one's full range of emotions (love or hate) and soulful commitment is the only way to experience life's best feeling and closest relationship to what God had in mind when creating humans. Even true love has its consequences. We can never predict the premature death, illness, un-requitement, disappointment, or a bevy of other unforeseen circumstances that might 'test' our love.

Given the choice of doing anything Pragmatically versus Passionately, I would strongly recommend doing something for Passionate reasons whenever possible. This, most importantly, would apply one's choice of career work or profession. In fact, which might be the way a profession is differentiated from a career. A passionate **choice** that is made irrespective of such practical reasons as salary, location, prestige, title, status, power, etc. In other words, something that one would willingly choose to spend one's life doing if money were no object. I am not talking about "starving for one's art" here but a work that you would love so much that you would do for free. For me, I made and can make double the money plying my talents on the corporate side than I do in academia. To me...the difference is as stark as the difference between having sex and making love!

I think life's most valuable skills are never taught formally in any class or course. Being FLEXIBLE, ADJUSTABLE, VARIABLE, ADAPTABLE, VERSATILE, AGILE, RESPONSE-ABLE (not react-able), and CREATIVE will be a lot more helpful in overcoming all of life's Challenges and/or capitalizing on all of life's Opportunities than most of the specific, academic, or technical skills we acquire in school.

The World is obsessed with data, statistics, stories, myths, information, research, news, and the like. Those efforts suggest that the highest order for people is knowledge, which has been proven repeatedly to be inaccurate, incomplete, untimely, or downright false (E.g., the atom is the smallest item of matter). That is why there is not much "wisdom" guiding neither by our leaders nor our organizations. As humans, we need to concentrate our efforts on our own individual, honest, pure, precious, genuine, authentic, sincere, and intrinsic "truth" and **not** let all the extrinsic 'noise' affect us very much at all!

Expectations are not as much 'bars' to be raised or lowered but more of 'silos' made of glass walls. The World just loves to put each one of us in narrowly defined categories designed to produce a desired result for that World. Not to suggest a "conspiracy theory" or anything, but rather individuals are being classified as little more than practical 'cogs' in the industrial/military/political/economic complex…UNLESS one does not fully cooperate. Using myself as an example (Like Jackson Browne wrote: "because I don't know about anyone but me"), I have 3 major life events which required going on my own 'road' less (never) travelled:

☙After working diligently for 20 years to become the Chief Marketing Officer of a major American Iconic Corporation, most people would have felt a tremendous sense of accomplishment having reached a pinnacle of one's career. But I felt empty and hollow. Being uncomfortable with that feeling prompted me to keep searching for more answers. Despite being a minority of one, my gut instincts told me not to settle, have absolutely NO regrets and to remain open to any and all possibilities. Four years later, I 'emerged' with my Doctorate and in retrospect, my instincts have been confirmed with what was obviously a wise career move. I take no credit other than being willing to be openly 'guided' by a variety of positive forces.

❧Despite not being blessed with children at an age when many would be expecting grandchildren, my 'masculine' intuition never stopped telling me that I was destined to be a Father. Ignoring 100% of others' advice, my perception of myself as a "Dad" would not cease. Three (challenging) kids later, my intuition has proven to be correct. I truly was meant to have children (despite a steep learning curve) and they are the best thing that EVER happened to me…so far!

❧Finally, at 45 years old, I participated in a clinical trial, (at a major University Research Teaching Hospital), of a study comparing biological age versus chronological age. I knew that I had rather good "longevity" in my family and valued health very much but was nevertheless shocked when my Biological age came in at 30 years of age. The researchers were also surprised as evidenced by the fact that they had me come back to check my mitochondria TWICE. Since then, I have followed the lifestyle advice of the LIFE EXTENSION Institute and continued to live my life (Doctoral Career, Wonderful Children and even, Late-in-Life Mortgage) like I have with at least 15 years of 'house' life expectancy to 'play with'.

If I had listened to the World's 'advice,' I would have become **NOTH-ING** of the person that I believe I have become and that I was **MEANT** to be! Thanks for <u>nothing</u> world! ;-D

Everybody knows the expression "Doing the <u>same</u> thing and expecting different results is the definition of "insanity." The real problem as I see it is that most people do not think they are doing the "same" thing when, in fact, they REALLY are. They may look for inconsequential differences (I.e., internal rationalizations) that really do not change anything. For example, one might continue to eat 'snowflakes' because no two are **exactly** the same. True, but the real lesson of insanity is: NOT to eat 'yellow' snow, no matter the (slight, insignificant) differences of the individual flakes! Forrest for the Trees?

The trouble with being "guarded" (self-protecting, 'wall'-building) is that, while defending oneself against the hurt that may come in from letting one's true self OUT, unfortunately, none of the good, healing 'stuff' (E.g., love) can get in. It is just like a lobster trap.

CON-CLUE-SION

Leadership Needs to be the NEW Management for the Future

An age old question has been: Is Leadership Born or Made? The <u>only</u> answer is a resounding YES! We are most certainly living in an era of Managers (NO Leaders) whose motivations are self-serving, ethics are suspect, communications are polarizing, and behaviors are 'transactional,' NOT "Transformative." I've tried to suggest some possible explanations why this may exist due to underlying 'realities' of Human Nature, Human Gender, Natural Geography, Political Power, Educational Pragmatism, Financial Considerations, Religious Postures, Historical References, Technological Developments and Spiritual Possibilities. No answers, no solutions, just food for thought. But hopefully not just "Meat and Potatoes" but a couple of 'delicacies' not often consumed. After all, is not **"controversy"** the 'spice' of ideation?

Since the idea of the "Great Man Theory" of Leaders being **born** has become outmoded, we must focus more on the 'behaviors' of people and not merely the 'traits' of their birth. Although, I would dare to say that **"made"** Leadership begins at birth, it is <u>not</u> mainly genetic. All children must be reared in environments where things like dignity, honor, integrity, trust, honesty, truth, and morality are treasured above all else. Everyone coming in contact with children can make positive contributions to the process of Leadership 'making' through a thousand little influences and impacts. So, in a way, parents, teachers, clergy, coaches, trainers, writers and all adults can be Leaders of the "village" necessary to raise up future generations. One does not have to be CEO, President, Chairman, Governor, Senator, or Mayor to add to the Leadership "collective."

From that universe of psychologically balanced, sociologically collaborative/cooperative, spiritually enlightened, emotionally healthy, and critical thinking adults may eventually emerge the Leader to take us from our current cultural morass to a proverbial 'promised land.' One thing for sure is that the rest of the "contributors" would certainly be better evolved for having been heavily invested in the aforementioned "village."

I can remember a very poignant juxtaposition of Management and Leadership from my days in the corporate arena. The Ford Pinto had a design flaw which may have caused the gas tank to explode and catch fire in the case of a rear-end collision. As I understand it, the Management at Ford "crunched the numbers" and decided that it made more <u>business sense</u> to pay the damages for any lawsuits than to incur the higher calculated costs of recalling all Pintos and fixing all of the problem with retrofitted gas tanks. They did not consider the unintended consequences of the public backlash to the publicity 'nightmare' of Ford choosing profits over the images of helpless people (especially car-seated children) burning to death in the backseats of those cars. A strong Management rationalization but not a scintilla of Leadership. It took the world about a decade for consumers to stop 'punishing' Ford through tremendous lost sales/profits.

In another situation around the same time, a small number of people in Chicago died when poisoned by someone 'meddling' with Tylenol bottles. This was at a time before safety-sealed, tamper-resistant packaging was the norm (come think about, this was probably the impetus for such packaging changes). The Leadership of McNeil Labs/Johnson and Johnson immediately removed EVERY bottle of Tylenol from EACH location, destroyed all the contents and replaced them with new, protective packaging bottles. A Leadership decision at its finest that did not concern itself with any short-term profits but only the long- term welfare of all potential consumers of its products. They have been rewarded for that demonstration of Leadership with great customer loyalty and company success since then.

You need to look no further than these two examples to comprehend the difference between Leadership and Management. A long-term, big-picture remedy for the many instead of a short-term 'bandage' for the relative few.

This is not to say that these two companies are either horrible or perfect, rather it describes the ongoing Herculean struggles individuals face between nearly impossible Leadership and Management organizational solution choices. And the consequences of each type of action.

While we are all waiting to 'grow' the next generation of potential Leaders, what must we consider and best focus upon? First of all, the idea of getting 100% of what any one individual wants in such a well-educated, well-informed, and well-to-do society is sheer lunacy. The goal should be more like an 80% consensus target as a more realistic place to begin any negotiation. Secondly, any prospective Leader needs to evaluate the world as it really IS (Unbelievable Complicated) and NOT as it WAS (WASPy Male Dominated) or would like it to BE (Perfectly Diverse/Inclusive/Equitable). I realized that it is incredible challenging to digest such complexity especially after 100 years of having OUR way by being the biggest, baddest 'dog' on the (world) 'block'.

Just like every personal change must begin with an admission of one's own actual objective self, I think the best place to start getting our country's 'house' in order is with an "America First" perspective. Not an American ONLY isolationist perception but a rearranged proportion of national priorities. Those depicted on the back cover of this book as a start for example. Just as bullet-proof vests protect our vital-organs "core" due to its critical importance to our overall survival, we must first protect the most vital resource that we have…the vital "core" of American people (I.e., Working people and families). Instead of the appendages of extreme positions (I.e., "elites") flailing around aimlessly, let's get back to basics. I.e., Our hearts are more important than our hands and feet. As such, we need to be as good customers as we are providers; as good clients as we are practitioners; and as good patients as we are professionals.

As a Constitutional Republic, we were created on the basis of the priorities of the people (the core). The essential components of Democratic Government, Capitalistic Economy and Christian Principles of America's creation have served us well for going on three hundred years. Are we ready to bail on those founding values just yet? As has been said, WE are not a perfect government (society?), but the best found so far. Besides, with the mechanism of "Amendments" we can always make any changes that are deemed better for the core of citizens.

As I see it, the largest single threat to the American Way of Life for its Citizens is the National Debt. With no plan to curtail the annual Deficit spending, it is inevitable that this Debt will crush future generations. If this were a Business arena instead of a Political one, Strategic Plans would be developed for a 20-year period to attack and conquer this issue. A multi-faceted, mani-pronged program would be needed with 'targets' to be hit, progress to be measured and accountability to be had. This problem is not being handled by Business minds nor Leadership direction. Rather, Political Managers have been ignoring/avoiding this situation and therefore, it is a catastrophe just waiting to happen. Fair, equitable, and even-handed solutions must be developed which both cut spending and add revenue. This must be addressed across the entire population whereby EVERYONE makes the 'sacrifices' necessary to the degree in which each can 'handle.' The vision and fortitude required to deal with this dire situation seems well beyond the capabilities of any people in current positions. Without addressing this situation, historians may point to this as the BIGGEST of the many reasons that the United States followed the dissolution of previous civilizations like Greece and Rome. Those reasons being that as a nation, we could not determine/distinguish who among us was really and truly in need nor those who could not put any self-imposed restrictions upon profiteering for their infinite greed.

How can we have HUNDREDS of BILLIONS of dollars for Foreign causes and yet not solve our most pressing problems at home? Has there ever been larger treachery than at our southern border or more crime on our big city streets? Would any of you reading this **starve** your family while feeding your acquaintances? Of course not! Yet that is exactly what Big Pharma, and the Industrial-Military complex is asking us to do. That is not Leadership but rather Governmental corruption apparently at the highest level. The Mismanagement of governmental positions has never been worse in my recollection and never has had more deleterious effects on a larger number of people. It is literally squeezing the once burgeoning middle class of society into an 'hourglass' shape.

Is there any benefit to our **Core Culture** for the tremendous influx of illegal drugs into our society? Is the ever-increasing homeless population beneficial to any city or town? Is energy dependence upon unfriendly nations superior to our own energy self-sufficiency? Does a never-ending negative balance from import/export payments help the upward mobility for future American Dreamers? Does isolating parents from their children's education experience strengthen family cohesiveness? Does rampant violent crime address everyone's primary psychological need for Safety & Security (according to Abraham Maslow)? I think it is obvious that all of these questions are rhetorical at best and ridiculous at worst. Yet, these are the extremely critical issues as to HOW the lack of Leadership in this country has failed us miserably. The other questions are unimaginably WHY? and WHEN? is the critical American **Core** going to <u>stop</u> taking it up the butt and <u>start</u> doing something about it? To me this is the very stuff that Revolutions are made of, including our own from the British Empire.

I believe the non-specific, ideological answer came from the wisdom of my 96-year-old Grandfather's own "Truth". He often likened the American society to that of an adolescent male and Italy to the wise, old, life master. Much like the arrogant teenager who projects his 'limited' experience over the rest of entirety, America is fond of telling places like Persia and China "how it all really is." Just as the teen who discovers some minor, commonly held information, America can often think that things must be "their way or the highway." Youth enables people to "burn the candle at both ends" with few or no consequences in the same manner in which America wastefully uses up its resources with little concern for the future outcomes. Adolescents have the speed and power to quicky recover from impetuous actions and rash decisions but not necessarily with any Common Sense at all. Invincibility and invulnerability are delusions of youth in much the same way The United States carries itself. Grandpa saw America as a gawky, pimple-faced kid that was way out over his (yes, a male) skis. In summary, a totally ego-self-centered perspective that is quite unrealistic.

Most adolescents grow 'up' and mature as they grow 'older,' however. This current "tipping" point will determine whether America grows gracefully, becomes an obnoxious adult, or never lives long enough to even find out?

Since many have said that "THE Business of America is BUSINESS," none of this lack of Leadership should be surprising at all. Since Financially oriented professionals are called "Money Managers" not Money Leaders, I would expect most Politically motivated people would be more concerned/focused on being the best Managers that they could and do things like planning, organizing, evaluating, controlling and only decisions which improve the short-term 'bottom line.' I might go as far as to say that Leadership is antithetical to maximizing business success as measured by that bottom line. As long as our priorities are materialistic in nature and not ideological we are destined to have tangible rewards (they who accumulate the most 'toys' wins) on earth and will not be living in peace in this life and maybe not truly "resting in peace" ever.

Since I believe that too much money is the 'root' of all Management and the lack of all Leadership, it seems to me that when all "millionaires" became "billionaires," our culture began its precipitous descent. While Gordon Gecko (in the original movie "Wall Street") thought that "Greed is Good," it was to a degree that allowed for the rich to provide an overall economy that supported healthy government Leadership for all. Politics and its pursuit of more and more Power seems contrary and counterproductive to any kind of Benevolent Leadership. No one seems to resist the temptation to submit to the old adage "Absolute Power Corrupts Absolutely." The excessive wealth that exists today is blinding, distorting and unhealthy in that all time and effort is spent Managing that wealth and no time or interest remains for Diplomacy, Statesmanship, Negotiation, or Compromise. In a word, Leadership.

Since I am not suggesting that anyone or anything can stop the world from its progressive 'spinning,' the ONLY thing that we can control is our inner selves. The good news is that is a GREAT place to start. Once we understand that the Global "elites" and "engineers" of the world are spending more effort (than we can possibly combat) creating 'features' (which we do not need but cannot avoid) when most of us just want real life 'benefits,' then and only then can we begin to resist the temptation to listen to the destructive 'tunes' of those 'pied pipers.' No one individual can find solace from the outside inward, only from the inside outward. The even better news is everyone's God lives WITHIN them and speaks to us all but in a soft/low voice. A voice that easily gets drown out by the noises of our 'outer' world unless we really focus our full attention with **active listening**. Followers had never been better prepared to follow a good Leader when one emerges but in the meantime, the only Leader we have comes from within through our "higher power," "conscience," "inner voice," "intuition," or "gut instincts." Above all, always think for yourself…AND…Critically!

In a phrase, we all need to rediscover our own individual God with the intention of saving our collective soul because, the truth is, whether we are conscious of it or not, that for each and every one of us:

<u>IN GOD WE THIRST!</u>

ABOUT THE AUTHOR

"Dr. Joe" Aniello is a tenured, full-professor at Francis Marion University in Florence, South Carolina.

He has taught in their School of Business for the last 21 years primarily in Organizational Leadership and Human Resource Behavior. He also has served as Executive Director of the Francis Marion University Center for Entrepreneurship and Small Business Management.

He holds an MBA in Marketing from Fordham University in New York City and an Education Doctorate from Vanderbilt University in Nashville, TN. His dissertation is on "Increasing Creativity in Adults."

Prior to his Academic Career, "Dr. Joe" spent over 20 years in major American Corporations rising to the level of Officer/Vice President.

He lives in Florence with his wife, Tracy, and their three young children: Elizabeth, Patrick, and Mary.

He has two great siblings, Anthony, his wife Sheila, and their children Autumn and Christian. Anne Marie Guerrero, her husband Danny and their children Jenna and Katie. Those families are all growing and flourishing.

Joe also had two awesome parents, Anthony F., and Antoinette Marie who have since gone on to their eternal rewards given for lives devoted to others. His parents continue to become even more awesome to me with each passing year of my life.